COACHING STOCK

FORTY-EIGHTH EDITION
2024

The complete guide to all
Locomotive-Hauled Carriages which
operate on the national railway network

R

GW00686371

SBN 978 1915 984 10 4

© 2023. Platform 5 Publishing Ltd, 52 Broadfield Road, Sheffield, S8 0XJ,
England.

Printed in England by The Lavenham Press, Lavenham, Suffolk.

CONTENTS

PROVISION OF INFORMATION

This book has been compiled with care to be as accurate as possible but some information is not easily available and the publisher cannot be held responsible for any errors or omissions. We would like to thank the companies and individuals who have been helpful in supplying information to us. The authors of this series of books are always pleased to receive notification of any inaccuracies that may be found, to enhance future editions. Please send comments to:

Robert Pritchard, Platform 5 Publishing Ltd, 52 Broadfield Road, Sheffield S8 0XJ, England.

e-mail: robert.pritchard@platform5.com Tel: 0114 255 2625.

This book is updated to information received by 16 October 2023.

UPDATES

This book is updated to the Stock Changes given in **Today's Railways UK 26?** (November 2023). The Platform 5 railway magazine "**Today's Railways UK** publishes Stock Changes every month to update this book. The magazine also contains news and rolling stock information on the railways of Great Britain and is published on the second Monday of every month. For further details of **Today's Railways UK**, please contact Platform 5 Publishing Ltd or visit our website **www.platform5.com**.

Front cover photograph: LNER oxblood-liveried Mark 4 Open Standard 1242 is seen at Peterborough on 7 May 2023.   **Ian Beards?**

BRITAIN'S RAILWAY SYSTEM

The structure of Britain's railway system has changed significantly during recent years, following the ongoing Covid-19 pandemic and subsequent drop in passenger numbers. Although passengers have since been returning in numbers, that drop in passengers in 2020 meant that franchises were no longer profitable and the Government was forced to step in and provide financial support to operators. Initially in March 2020 the Transport Secretary suspended rail franchising and operators transitioned to "Emergency Measures Agreements". These EMAs suspended the normal financial agreements, instead transferring all revenue and cost risk to the Government. Operators in England all accepted these new arrangements and continued to operate trains (initially with reduced service frequencies) for a small management fee. Similar arrangements were put in place by the Scottish and Welsh Governments for ScotRail, Caledonian Sleeper and Transport for Wales.

The EMAs initially lasted for six months from which time longer "Emergency Recovery Management Agreements" (ERMAs) were put in place. These were similar management contracts which continued to see operators run services for a management fee. Since then operators have been transitioning to new National Rail Contracts (NRCs). During an NRC operators are paid a fixed management fee of around 1.5% for operating services and additional small performance fees if agreed targets are achieved.

In the longer term a new body called Great British Railways is planned to take over the running of the railways and specifically take over Network Rail's responsibilities as well as some functions currently carried out by the Department for Transport and Rail Delivery Group. The franchise model will be changed to one of concessions, although this will take some years to fully implement.

In London and on Merseyside concessions were already in place. These see the operator paid a fee to run the service, within tightly specified guidelines. Operators running a concession would not normally take commercial risks, although there are usually penalties and rewards in the contract.

Britain's national railway infrastructure is owned by a "not for dividend" company, Network Rail. In 2014 Network Rail was reclassified as a public sector company, being described by the Government as a "public sector arm's-length body of the Department for Transport".

Most stations and maintenance depots are leased to and operated by the Train Operating Companies (TOCs), but some larger stations are controlled by Network Rail. The only exception is the infrastructure on the Isle of Wight: The Island Line franchise uniquely included maintenance of the infrastructure as well as the operation of passenger services. Both the infrastructure and trains are operated by South Western Railway.

Trains are operated by TOCs over Network Rail tracks (termed the National Network), regulated by access agreements between the parties involved. In general, TOCs are responsible for the provision and maintenance of the trains and staff necessary for the direct operation of services, whilst

Network Rail is responsible for the provision and maintenance of the infrastructure and also for staff to regulate the operation of services.

The Department for Transport (DfT) is the authority for the national network. Transport Scotland has operated ScotRail since April 2022 and is also responsible for the Caledonian Sleeper franchises. In February 2021 the Welsh Government took over the operation of the Wales & Borders franchise (Transport for Wales) from KeolisAmey.

Each franchise was set up with the right to run specified services within a specified area for a period of time, in return for the right to charge fares and, where appropriate, to receive financial support from the Government. Subsidy was payable in respect of socially necessary services. Service standards are monitored by the DfT throughout the duration of the franchise. Franchisees earned revenue primarily from fares and from subsidy. They generally leased stations from Network Rail and earned rental income by sub-letting parts of them, for example to retailers.

TOC's and open access operator's main costs are the track access charges they pay to Network Rail, the costs of leasing stations and rolling stock and of employing staff. Franchisees may do light maintenance work on rolling stock or contract it out to other companies. Heavy maintenance is normally carried out by the Rolling Stock Leasing Companies, according to contracts.

DOMESTIC PASSENGER TRAIN OPERATORS

The majority of passenger trains are operated by Train Operating Companies, now supported by the Government through National Rail Contracts. For reference the date of the expiry of the original franchise is also given here (if later than the current NRC expiry date).

Name of franchise	Operator	Trading Name
Caledonian Sleeper	Scottish Government	**Caledonian Sleeper**

The original Sleeper franchise started in April 2015 when operation of the ScotRail and ScotRail Sleeper franchises was separated. Abellio won the ScotRail franchise and Serco the Caledonian Sleeper franchise. The Scottish Government took over the operation of the Sleeper from Abellio in 2023. Caledonian Sleeper operates four trains nightly between London Euston and Scotland using locomotives hired from GBRf. New CAF Mark 5 rolling stock was introduced during 2019.

Chiltern	Arriva (Deutsche Bahn)	**Chiltern Railways**

NRC until 1 April 2025 with the option to extend to December 2027

Chiltern Railways operates a frequent service between London Marylebone, Oxford, Banbury and Birmingham Snow Hill, with some peak trains extending to Kidderminster. There are also regular services from Marylebone to Stratford-upon-Avon and to Aylesbury Vale Parkway via Amersham (along the London Underground Metropolitan Line). The fleet consists of DMUs of Classes 165, and 168 plus a number of locomotive-hauled rakes used on some of the Birmingham route trains, worked by Class 68s hired from DRS.

Cross Country Arriva (Deutsche Bahn) **CrossCountry**
ERMA until 15 October 2027 with the option to extend to October 2031

CrossCountry operates a network of long distance services between Scotland, the North-East of England and Manchester to the South-West of England, Reading, Southampton, Bournemouth and Guildford, centred on Birmingham New Street. These trains are formed of diesel Class 220/221 Voyagers. Inter-urban services also link Nottingham, Leicester and Stansted Airport with Birmingham and Cardiff. These trains use Class 170 DMUs.

Crossrail MTR **Elizabeth Line**
Concession until 27 May 2025

This concession started in May 2015. Initially Crossrail took over the Liverpool Street–Shenfield stopping service from Greater Anglia, using a fleet of Class 315 EMUs, with the service branded "TfL Rail". The core Crossrail railway in central London started operating in May 2022 and since then the operation has been branded the "Elizabeth Line". Class 345 EMUs are now used on all services running from Reading/Heathrow Airport to Shenfield/Abbey Wood.

East Coast DfT **London North Eastern Railway**
Operated by DfT's "Operator of Last Resort" until June 2025

LNER operates frequent long distance trains on the East Coast Main Line between London King's Cross, Leeds, Lincoln, Harrogate, York, Newcastle-upon-Tyne and Edinburgh, with less frequent services to Bradford, Skipton, Hull, Middlesbrough, Glasgow, Stirling, Aberdeen and Inverness. A fleet of 65 Hitachi Class 800 and 801 "Azuma" trains (a mix of bi-mode and electric, 5- and 9-car units) operate the majority of services. A small number of Class 91+Mark 4 sets have been retained and are mainly used on Leeds and some York services.

East Midlands Transport UK Group **East Midlands Railway**
NRC until 17 October 2026 with the option to extend to October 2030

EMR operates a mix of long distance high speed services on the Midland Main Line (MML), from London St Pancras to Sheffield, Nottingham (plus peak-hour trains to Lincoln) and Corby, and local and regional services ranging from the long distance Norwich–Liverpool route to Nottingham–Skegness, Nottingham–Mansfield–Worksop, Derby–Matlock and Newark Castle–Crewe. It also operates local services across Lincolnshire. Trains on the MML are worked by a fleet of Class 222 DMUs, whilst the local and regional fleet consists of DMU Classes 158 and 170. Class 360 EMUs operate services on the St Pancras–Corby route.

East Anglia Transport UK Group (60%)/Mitsui Group (40%) **Greater Anglia**
NRC until 19 September 2024 with option for a 2 year extension; original franchise was until 11 October 2025

Greater Anglia operates main line trains between London Liverpool Street, Ipswich and Norwich and local trains across Norfolk, Suffolk and parts of Cambridgeshire. It also runs local and commuter services into Liverpool Street from the Great Eastern (including Southend, Braintree and Clacton) and West Anglia (including Ely/Cambridge and Stansted Airport) routes. In 2019–20 a new fleet of Stadler EMUs and bi-mode units (Classes 745 and 755) was introduced on the GEML and in East Anglia, replacing older DMUs and loco-hauled trains. A large fleet of 133 new 5-car Class 720 Aventras now all other services out of Liverpool Street.

Essex Thameside Trenitalia **c2c**
NRC until 25 July 2025; original franchise was until 10 November 2029

c2c operates an intensive, principally commuter, service from London Fenchurch Street to Southend and Shoeburyness, via both Upminster and Tilbury. The fleet consists of 74 Class 357 EMUs and a fleet of 12 new 5-car Class 720 Aventras.

Great Western   First Group   **Great Western Railway**
NRC until 21 June 2025 with the option to extend to June 2028

Great Western Railway operates long distance trains from London Paddington to South Wales, the West Country and Worcester and Hereford. In addition, there are frequent trains along the Thames Valley corridor to Newbury/Bedwyn and Oxford, plus local and regional trains throughout the South-West including the Cornish, Devon and Thames Valley branches, the Reading–Gatwick North Downs Line and Cardiff–Portsmouth Harbour and Bristol–Weymouth regional routes. Long distance services are in the hands of a fleet of Class 800/802 bi-mode InterCity Express Trains. DMUs of Classes 165 and 166 are used on the Thames Valley branches and North Downs routes as well as on local services around Bristol and Exeter and across to Cardiff. Class 387 EMUs are used between Paddington, Reading, Didcot Parkway and Newbury. Classes 150, 158, 165 and 166 and a small fleet of short 4-car HSTs are used on local and regional trains in the South-West. A small fleet of Class 57s is maintained to work the overnight "Cornish Riviera" Sleeper service between London Paddington and Penzance formed of Mark 3 coaches.

London Rail   Arriva (Deutsche Bahn)   **London Overground**
Concession until 3 May 2026

London Overground operates services on the Richmond–Stratford North London Line and the Willesden Junction–Clapham Junction West London Line, plus the East London Line from Highbury & Islington to New Cross and New Cross Gate, with extensions to Clapham Junction (via Denmark Hill), Crystal Palace and West Croydon. It also runs services from London Euston to Watford Junction. All these use Class 378 EMUs, with Class 710s also used on the Watford Junction route. Class 710s operate services on the Gospel Oak–Barking Riverside line. London Overground also operates some suburban services from London Liverpool Street – to Chingford, Enfield Town and Cheshunt. These services mainly use Class 710/1s, with one of these units additionally used on the Romford–Upminster shuttle.

Merseyrail Electrics   Serco (50%)/Transport UK Group (50%)   **Merseyrail**
Concession until 22 July 2028. Under the control of Merseytravel PTE instead of the DfT
Due to be reviewed every five years to fit in with the Merseyside Local Transport Plan

Merseyrail operates services between Liverpool and Southport, Ormskirk, Kirkby, Hunts Cross, New Brighton, West Kirby, Chester and Ellesmere Port. A new fleet of Class 777 EMUs are currently replacing the Class 507 and 508 EMUs.

Northern   DfT   **Northern**
Operated by DfT's "Operator of Last Resort" until further notice

Northern operates a range of inter-urban, commuter and rural services throughout the North of England, including those around the cities of Leeds, Manchester, Sheffield, Liverpool and Newcastle. The network extends from Chathill in the north to Nottingham in the south, and Cleethorpes in the east to St Bees in the west. Long distance services include Leeds–Carlisle, Morpeth–Carlisle and York–Blackpool North. The operator uses a large fleet of DMUs of Classes 150, 155, 156, 158, 170 and 195 plus EMU Classes 319, 323, 331 and 333. New fleets of DMUs (Class 195) and EMUs (Class 331) are used on a number of routes, and were followed by Class 769 bi-mode diesel electric units (converted from Class 319s) in 2021.

ScotRail   Scottish Government   **ScotRail**
Operated by the Scottish Government from April 2022, having taken over ScotRail from Abellio

ScotRail provides almost all passenger services within Scotland and also trains from Glasgow to Carlisle via Dumfries. The company operates a large fleet of DMUs of Classes 156, 158 and 170 and EMU Classes 318, 320, 334, 380 and 385. A fleet of 25 refurbished HSTs have been introduced onto InterCity services between Edinburgh/Glasgow and Aberdeen and Inverness and also between Inverness and Aberdeen. In 2021 five Class 153s were also introduced on the West Highland Line (mainly the Oban line) to provide more capacity and space for bikes and other luggage.

South Eastern	DfT	**Southeastern**

Operated by DfT's "Operator of Last Resort" until further notice.

Southeastern operates all services in the south-east London suburbs, the whole of Kent and part of Sussex, which are primarily commuter services to London. It also operates domestic High Speed trains on HS1 from London St Pancras to Ashford, Ramsgate, Dover and Faversham with additional peak services on other routes. EMUs of Classes 375, 376, 377, 465, 466 and 707 are used, along with Class 395s on the High Speed trains.

South Western	First Group (70%)/MTR (30%)	**South Western Railway**

NRC until 25 May 2025

South Western Railway operates trains from London Waterloo to destinations across the South and South-West including Woking, Basingstoke, Southampton, Portsmouth, Salisbury, Exeter, Reading and Weymouth, as well as suburban services from Waterloo. SWR also runs services between Ryde and Shanklin on the Isle of Wight, from November 2021 using a fleet of five third rail Vivarail Class 484 units (converted former LU D78 stock). The rest of the fleet consists of DMU Classes 158 and 159 and EMU Classes 444, 450, 455 and 458. A new fleet of Bombardier Class 701s are being delivered and should enter service from late 2023.

Thameslink, Southern &	Govia (Go-Ahead/Keolis)	**Govia Thameslink Railway**
Great Northern (TSGN)		

NRC until 1 April 2025 with the option to extend to April 2028

TSGN is the largest operator in Great Britain (the former Southern franchise was combined with Thameslink/Great Northern in 2015). GTR uses four brands: "Thameslink" for trains between Cambridge North, Peterborough, Bedford and Rainham, Sevenoaks, East Grinstead, Brighton, Littlehampton and Horsham via central London and also on the Sutton/Wimbledon loop using Class 700 EMUs. "Great Northern" comprises services from London King's Cross and Moorgate to Welwyn Garden City, Hertford North, Peterborough, Cambridge and King's Lynn using Class 387 and 717 EMUs. "Southern" operates predominantly commuter services between London, Surrey and Sussex and "metro" services in South London, as well as services along the south Coast between Southampton, Brighton, Hastings and Ashford, plus the cross-London service from South Croydon to Milton Keynes. Class 171 DMUs are used on Ashford–Eastbourne and London Bridge–Uckfield services, whilst all other services are in the hands of Class 377 and 700 EMUs. Finally, Gatwick Express operates semi-fast trains between London Victoria, Gatwick Airport and Brighton using Class 387/2 EMUs.

Trans-Pennine Express	DfT	**TransPennine Express**

Operated by DfT's "Operator of Last Resort" until further notice.

TransPennine Express operates predominantly long distance inter-urban services linking major cities across the North of England, along with Edinburgh and Glasgow in Scotland. The main services are Manchester Airport–Saltburn, Liverpool–Hull, Manchester Piccadilly–York–Scarborough and Liverpool–Newcastle/Edinburgh along the North Trans-Pennine route via Huddersfield, Leeds and York, and Liverpool–Manchester Piccadilly–Cleethorpes along the South Trans-Pennine route via Sheffield. TPE also operates Manchester Airport–Edinburgh/Glasgow and Liverpool–Glasgow services. The fleet consists of Class 185 DMUs, plus three new fleets: Class 68s+Mark 5A (which are to be withdrawn in December 2023) used on the Scarborough route, Class 397s used on Manchester Airport/Liverpool–Scotland and Class 802 bi-mode units used mainly on Liverpool–Newcastle/Edinburgh.

Wales & Borders   Welsh Government   **Transport for Wales**
From February 2021 the Welsh Government took direct control of rail service operation. Infrastructure management continues to be managed by KeolisAmey.

Transport for Wales was procured by the Welsh Government and operates a mix of long distance, regional and local services throughout Wales, including the Valley Lines network of lines around Cardiff, and also through services to the English border counties and to Manchester and Birmingham. The fleet consists of DMUs of Classes 150, 153, 158, 170 and 175 and locomotive-hauled Mark 4 sets hauled by Class 67s. Rebuilt Class 230 diesel-battery units are used on the Wrexham–Bidston line and new Stadler (Class 231/398/756) and CAF (Class 197) fleets are being introduced across other routes by 2025.

West Coast Partnership   First Group (70%)/Trenitalia (30%)   **Avanti West Coast**
NRC until 18 October 2026 with the option to extend to October 2032

Avanti West Coast operates long distance services along the West Coast Main Line from London Euston to Birmingham/Wolverhampton, Manchester, Liverpool, Blackpool North and Glasgow/Edinburgh using Class 390 Pendolino EMUs. It also operates Class 221 Voyagers on the Euston–Chester–Holyhead route and a small number of trains from Wolverhampton to Shrewsbury and to Wrexham. New Hitachi Class 805 and 807 units are due into service from 2024.

West Midlands Trains   Transport UK Group (70%)/JR East (15%)/**West Midlands Railway/**
Mitsui (15%)   **London Northwestern**
NRC until 19 September 2024 with option to extend to September 2026; original franchise ran until 31 March 2026

West Midlands Trains operates services under two brand names. West Midlands Railway trains are local and regional services around Birmingham, including to Stratford-upon-Avon, Worcester, Hereford, Redditch, Rugeley and Shrewsbury. WMR is managed by a consortium of 16 councils and the Department for Transport. London Northwestern is the brand used for long distance and regional services from London Euston to Northampton and Birmingham/Crewe and also between Birmingham and Liverpool, Bedford–Bletchley and Watford Junction–St Albans Abbey. The fleet consists of DMU Classes 139, 150 and 172 and EMU Classes 319, 323 and 350. New fleets of CAF Class 196 DMUs and Bombardier Class 730 EMUs are being introduced across a number of routes between 2022 and 2025.

NON-FRANCHISED SERVICES

The following operators run non-franchised, or "open access" services
(* special seasonal services):

Operator	Trading Name	Route
Heathrow Airport Holdings	Heathrow Express	London Paddington–Heathrow Airport

Heathrow Express is a frequent express passenger service between London Paddington and Heathrow Airport using a sub-fleet of Great Western Railway Class 387 EMUs (operated jointly with GWR).

Hull Trains (part of First)	Hull Trains	London King's Cross–Hull

Hull Trains operates seven trains a day on weekdays from Hull to London King's Cross via the East Coast Main Line. Bi-mode Class 802s were introduced in 2019–20. Two trains in each direction start back from and extend to Beverley.

Grand Central (part of Arriva)	Grand Central	London King's Cross–Sunderland/ Bradford Interchange

Grand Central operates five trains a day from Sunderland and four from Bradford Interchange to London King's Cross using Class 180 or 221 DMUs.

Locomotive Services (TOC)	Locomotive Services	

Locomotive Services runs various excursions across the network using diesel, electric and steam locomotives operating under the brands Saphos Trains (principally steam-hauled trips), Statesman Rail (diesel-locomotive hauled trips and land cruises), Rail Charter Services, Midland Pullman (HST tours using the luxury HST set) and Intercity (mainly electric locomotive-hauled tours).

First East Coast	Lumo	London King's Cross–Edinburgh

Lumo started operating services from London to Edinburgh via the East Coast Main Line in October 2021 and now operates five trains per day using new electric Class 803 units.

North Yorkshire Moors Railway Enterprises	North Yorkshire Moors Railway	Pickering–Grosmont–Whitby/ Battersby, Sheringham–Cromer*

The North Yorkshire Moors Railway operates services on the national network between Grosmont and Whitby as an extension of its Pickering–Grosmont services and also operates services between Sheringham and Cromer on behalf of the North Norfolk Railway.

South Yorkshire Supertram	Stagecoach Supertram	Meadowhall South–Rotherham Parkgate

South Yorkshire Supertram holds a passenger licence to allow the operation of the pilot tram-train service linking Sheffield city centre with Rotherham Central and Rotherham Parkgate.

Tyne & Wear PTE	Tyne & Wear Metro	Pelaw–Sunderland

Tyne & Wear Passenger Transport Executive holds a passenger license to allow the operation of its Metro service over Network Rail tracks between Pelaw and Sunderland.

Vintage Trains	Vintage Trains	Birmingham Snow Hill–Stratford-upon-Avon*

Vintage Trains operates steam-hauled services on a seasonal basis.

West Coast Railway Company	West Coast Railway Company	Fort William–Mallaig* York–Settle–Carlisle* Carnforth–York–Scarborough*

WCRC operates steam-hauled services on these routes on a seasonal basis and a range of other excursions across the network, including the Northern Belle luxury train.

INTERNATIONAL PASSENGER OPERATORS

Eurostar International operates passenger services between London St Pancras and mainland Europe. The company, established in 2010, is jointly owned by SNCF (the national operator of France): 55%, SNCB (the national operator of Belgium): 5% and Patina Rail: 40%. Patina Rail is made up of Canadian-based Caisse de dépôt et placement du Québec (CDPG) and UK-based Hermes Infrastructure (owning 30% and 10% respectively). This 40% was previously owned by the UK Government until it was sold in 2015.

In addition, a service for the conveyance of accompanied road vehicles through the Channel Tunnel is provided by the tunnel operating company, Eurotunnel. All Eurotunnel services are operated in top-and-tail mode by the powerful Class 9 Bo-Bo-Bo locomotives.

FREIGHT TRAIN OPERATORS

The following operators operate freight services or empty passenger stock workings under "open access" arrangements:

Colas Rail
DB Cargo (UK)
Devon & Cornwall Railways (DCR)
Direct Rail Services
Freightliner
GB Railfreight
LORAM (UK)
Rail Adventure
Rail Operations Group
Varamis Rail
West Coast Railway Company

In addition, Amey, Balfour Beatty Rail, Harsco Rail, Swietelsky Babcock Rail (SB Rail) and VolkerRail operate trains formed of On-Track Machines.

INTRODUCTION

This book contains details of all locomotive-hauled or propelled coaching stock, often referred to as carriages, which can run on Britain's national railway network.

The number of locomotive-hauled or propelled carriages in use on the national railway network is much fewer than was once the case. Those that remain fall into two distinct groups.

Firstly, there are those used by franchised and open access operators for regular timetabled services. Today, most of these are formed in fixed or semi-fixed formations with either locomotives or a locomotive and Driving Brake Carriage at either end which allows for push-pull operation. There are also a small number of mainly overnight trains with variable formations which use conventional locomotive haulage.

Secondly, there are those used for what can best be described as excursion trains. These include a wide range of carriage types ranging from luxurious saloons to those more suited to the "bucket and spade" seaside type of excursion. These are formed into sets to suit the requirements of the day. From time to time some see limited use with franchised and open access operators to cover for stock shortages and times of exceptional demand such as major sporting events.

In addition, there remain a small number of carriages referred to as "Service Stock" which are used internally within the railway industry and are not used to convey passengers.

FRANCHISED & OPEN ACCESS OPERATORS

For each operator regularly using locomotive-hauled carriages brief details are given here of the sphere of operation. For details of operators using HSTs see Section 2.

Caledonian Sleeper
This franchise, operated by Serco until June 2023, started in 2015 when the Anglo-Scottish Sleeper operation was split from the ScotRail franchise. Caledonian Sleeper operates seating and sleeping car services between London Euston and Scotland using sets of new CAF Mark 5 Sleeping Cars and seated carriages.

GBRf is contracted to supply the motive power for the Sleepers. Class 92s are used between London Euston and Edinburgh/Glasgow Central and rebuilt Class 73/9s between Edinburgh and Inverness, Aberdeen and Fort William, with Class 66s assisting as required, usually on the Inverness or Fort William legs.

Chiltern Railways
Chiltern operates four sets of Mark 3 carriages hauled by DRS Class 68 locomotives on its Mainline services between London Marylebone and Birmingham Moor Street/Kidderminster. Trains operate as push-pull sets.

Great Western Railway
The "Night Riviera" seating and sleeping car service between London Paddington and Penzance uses sets of Mark 3 carriages hauled by Class 57/6 locomotives.

London North Eastern Railway
LNER has retained eight rakes of Mark 4 carriages and these are hauled by Class 91 locomotives in push-pull formation on a number of InterCity services mainly between London King's Cross and Leeds or York. All other services on the East Coast Main Line are in the hands of LNER's fleet of 65 "Azuma" bi-mode or electric units.

North Yorkshire Moors Railway
In addition to operating the North Yorkshire Moors Railway between Pickering and Grosmont the company operates through services to Whitby. A fleet of Mark 1 passenger carriages and Pullman Cars are used for these services. It also operates the "North Norfolkman" services on behalf of the North Norfolk Railway between Sheringham and Cromer.

TransPennine Express
TPE has 13 sets of new CAF Mark 5A coaches that were originally due to enter service in 2019 but due to teething problems and delays with crew training have never been fully introduced and are now planned to be withdrawn in December 2023. The sets are used on some services on the Manchester/York–Scarborough route They are operated using DRS Class 68s in push-pull mode.

Transport for Wales
TfW ceased using its Mark 3 rakes in March 2020. It took on lease three shortened rakes of ex-LNER Mark 4s and these were introduced in spring 2021 on the Cardiff–Holyhead route, in push-pull mode with Class 67s. TfW also purchased an additional five Mark 4 rakes (including four originally intended for use on Grand Central's Euston–Blackpool North service) that were introduced on the Manchester–Cardiff route from 2023, also using Class 67s. The sets initially operated in 4-car formation, but are being lengthened to five carriages during 2023–24.

West Coast Railway Company
WCRC operates two sets of Mark 1 or Mark 2 carriages on its regular steam-hauled "Jacobite" trains between Fort William and Mallaig. These trains normally operate between early April and late October.

EXCURSION TRAIN OPERATORS

Usually, three types of companies will be involved in the operation of an excursion train. There will be the promoter, the rolling stock provider and the train operator. In many cases two or more of these roles may be undertaken by the same or associated companies. Only a small number of Train Operating Companies facilitate the operation of excursion trains. This takes various forms ranging from the complete package of providing and operating the train, through offering a "hook up and haul" service, to operating the train for a third-party rolling stock custodian.

DB Cargo UK
DBC currently operates its own luxurious train of Mark 3 carriages, called the Company Train. It also offers a hook up and haul service and regularly operates the Royal Train and the Belmond British Pullman as well as trains for Riviera Trains and their client promoters.

Direct Rail Services
DRS has offered a hook up and haul service for Riviera Trains and its client promoters but has sold its own fleet of carriages.

GB Railfreight
GBRf initially operated excursion trains using the preserved Class 201 "Hastings" DEMU. It now also operates a small number of company excursions using hired-in carriages. The company also offers a hook up and haul service operating the Royal Scotsman luxury train, as well as trains for Riviera Trains and its client promoters.

Locomotive Services
This vertically integrated company gained an operating license in 2017. From its base at Crewe, excursion trains are operated across the country using its increasingly varied fleet of steam, diesel and electric locomotives and Mark 1/2/3 carriages, and also using the "Midland Pullman" HST set.

Rail Operations Group
This company has operated a small number of excursion trains using hired in carriages. It also offers a hook up and haul service.

Vintage Trains
This vertically integrated company gained a licence in 2018. From its base at Tyseley it operates the "Shakespeare Express" steam service between Birmingham and Stratford-upon-Avon. It also operates excursions using its fleet of steam and diesel locomotives and Mark 1/2 carriages and Pullman cars.

West Coast Railway Company
This vertically integrated company has its own large fleet of steam and diesel locomotives as well as a full range of different carriage types. It operates its own regular trains, including the luxury Northern Belle, the "Jacobite" steam service between Fort William and Mallaig, the "Dalesman" steam and diesel services over the Settle & Carlisle route and numerous excursion trains for itself and client promoters. In addition, it offers a hook up and haul service operating trains for companies such as The Princess Royal Locomotive Trust and the Scottish Railway Preservation Society.

LAYOUT OF INFORMATION

Carriages are listed in numerical order of painted number in batches according to type.

Where a carriage has been renumbered, the former number is shown in parentheses. If a carriage has been renumbered more than once, the original number is shown first, followed by the most recent previous number.

Each carriage entry is laid out as in the following example (previous number(s) column may be omitted where not applicable):

No.	Prev. No.	Notes	Livery	Owner	Operator	Depot/Location
82301	(82117)	g	**CM**	AV	CR	AL

Codes: Codes are used to denote the livery, owner, operator and depot/location of each carriage. Details of codes used can be found in Section 10 of this book.

The owner is the responsible custodian of the carriage and this may not always be the legal owner. Actual ownership can be very complicated. Some vehicles are owned by finance/leasing companies. Others are owned by subsidiary companies of a holding company or by an associate company of the responsible custodian or operator.

The operator is the organisation which facilitates the use of the carriage and may not be the actual train operating company which runs the train. If no operator is shown the carriage is considered to be not in use.

The depot is the facility primarily responsible for the carriages maintenance. Light maintenance and heavy overhauls may also be carried out elsewhere.

The location is where carriages not in use are currently being kept or are stored.

GENERAL INFORMATION

CLASSIFICATION AND NUMBERING

Seven different numbering systems were in use on British Rail. These were the British Rail series, the four pre-nationalisation companies' series', the Pullman Car Company's series and the UIC (International Union of Railways) series. In this book BR number series carriages and former Pullman Car Company series are listed separately. There is also a separate listing of "Saloon" type carriages, that includes pre-nationalisation survivors, which are permitted to run on the national railway system, Locomotive Support Carriages and Service Stock. Please note the Mark 2 Pullman carriages were ordered after the Pullman Car Company had been nationalised and are therefore numbered in the British Rail series. The new CAF Mark 5/Mark 5A carriages have been allocated numbers in the British Rail series.

Also listed separately are the British Rail and Pullman Car Company number series carriages used on North Yorkshire Moors Railway and North Norfolk Railway services on very limited parts of the national railway network. This is due to their very restricted sphere of operation.

The BR number series grouped carriages of a particular type together in chronological order. Major modifications affecting type of accommodation resulted in renumbering into a more appropriate or new number series. Since privatisation such renumbering has not always taken place, resulting in renumbering which has been more haphazard and greater variations within numbering groups.

With the introduction of the TOPS numbering system, coaching stock (including multiple unit vehicles) retained their original BR number unless this conflicted with a locomotive number. Carriages can be one–five digits, although no one or two-digit examples remain in use on the national network. BR generally numbered "Service Stock" in a six-digit wagon number series.

UNITS OF MEASUREMENT

All dimensions and weights are quoted for carriages in an "as new" condition or after a major modification, such as fitting with new bogies etc. Dimensions are quoted in the order length x width. Lengths quoted are over buffers or couplers as appropriate. All widths quoted are maxima. All weights are shown as metric tonnes (t = tonnes).

DIMENSIONS

Carriage lengths are summarised as follows:

Mark 1: 19.35 m or 17.37 m.
Mark 2: 19.66 m.
Mark 3: 23.00 m.
Mark 3 HST: 23.00 m.

Mark 4: 23.00 m.
Mark 5: 22.20 m.
Mark 5A: 22.20–22.37 m.

DETAILED INFORMATION & CODES

Under each type heading, the following details are shown:

- "Mark" of carriage (see below).
- Descriptive text.
- Number of First Class seats, Standard Class seats, lavatory compartments and wheelchair spaces shown as F/S nT nW respectively. A number in brackets indicates tip-up seats (in addition to the regular seats).
- Bogie type (see below).
- Additional features.
- ETS Index.
- Weight: All weights are shown as metric tonnes.

BOGIE TYPES

Gresley. LNER design of bogie first used in the "Gresley" era. Used by BR on some Mark 1 catering carriages. Now used for some saloons.

BR Mark 1 (BR1). Double bolster leaf spring bogie. Generally 90 mph, but Mark 1 bogies may be permitted to run at 100 mph with special maintenance. Weight: 6.1 t.

BR Mark 2 (BR2). Single bolster leaf-spring bogie used on certain types of non-passenger stock and suburban stock (all now withdrawn). Weight: 5.3 t.

COMMONWEALTH (C). Heavy, cast steel coil spring bogie. 100 mph. Weight: 6.75 t.

B4. Coil spring fabricated bogie. Generally 100 mph, but B4 bogies may be permitted to run at 110 mph with special maintenance. Weight: 5.2 t.

B5. Heavy duty version of B4. 100 mph. Weight: 5.3 t.

B5 (SR). A bogie originally used on Southern Region EMUs, similar in design to B5. Now also used on locomotive-hauled carriages. 100 mph.

BT10. A fabricated bogie designed for 125 mph. Air suspension.

T4. A 125 mph bogie designed by BREL (now Bombardier Transportation).

BT41. Fitted to Mark 4 carriages, designed by SIG in Switzerland. At present limited to 125 mph, but designed for 140 mph.

CAF. Fitted to CAF Mark 5 and Mark 5A carriages.

BRAKES

Air braking is now standard on British main line trains. Carriages with other equipment are denoted:

b   Air braked, through vacuum pipe.
v   Vacuum braked.
x   Dual braked (air and vacuum).

HEATING & VENTILATION

Electric heating and ventilation is now standard on British main-line trains. Certain carriages for use on excursion services may also have steam heating facilities, or be steam heated only. All carriages used on North Yorkshire Moors Railway and North Norfolk Railway trains have steam heating.

NOTES ON ELECTRIC TRAIN SUPPLY

The sum of ETS indices in a train must not be more than the ETS index of the locomotive or generator van. The normal voltage on British trains is 1000 V. Suffix "X" denotes 600 amp wiring instead of 400 amp. Trains whose ETS index is higher than 66 must be formed completely of 600 amp wired stock. Class 33 and 73/1 locomotives cannot provide a suitable electric train supply for Mark 2D, Mark 2E, Mark 2F, Mark 3, Mark 3A, Mark 3B or Mark 4 carriages. Class 55 locomotives provide an ETS directly from one of their traction generators into the train line. Consequently, voltage fluctuations can result in motor-alternator flashover. Thus these locomotives are not suitable for use with Mark 2D, Mark 2E, Mark 2F, Mark 3, Mark 3A, Mark 3B or Mark 4 carriages unless modified motor-alternators are fitted. Such motor alternators were fitted to Mark 2D and 2F carriages used on the East Coast Main Line, but few remain fitted.

PUBLIC ADDRESS

It is assumed all carriages are now fitted with public address equipment, although certain stored carriages may not have this feature. In addition, it is assumed all carriages with a conductor's compartment have public address transmission facilities, as have catering carriages.

COOKING EQUIPMENT

It is assumed that Mark 1 catering carriages have gas powered cooking equipment, whilst Mark 2, 3 and 4 catering carriages have electric powered cooking equipment unless stated otherwise.

ADDITIONAL FEATURE CODES

(+4) Indicates tip-up seats in that carriage (in addition to the fixed seats).
d   Central Door Locking.
dg   Driver–Guard communication equipment.
f   Facelifted or fluorescent lighting.
h   "High density" seating
k   Composition brake blocks (instead of cast iron).
n   Day/night lighting.
pg   Public address transmission and driver-guard communication.
pt   Public address transmission facility.
q   Catering staff to shore telephone.
T   Toilet
TD   A universal access toilet suitable for use by person of reduced mobility.
w   Wheelchair space.

More modern Mark 4 and Mark 5 carriages were fitted with retention toilets as built and most Mark 3s were later retrofitted with them (as have all HST vehicles that are still in regular passenger service). Mark 1, 2 and 3 charter stock still used on the main line have mainly now been fitted with retention toilets.

BUILD DETAILS

Lot Numbers
Vehicles ordered under the auspices of BR were allocated a lot (batch) number when ordered and these are quoted in class headings and sub-headings.

Builders
These are shown in class headings, the following designations being used:

Ashford	BR, Ashford Works.
BRCW	Birmingham Railway Carriage & Wagon Company, Smethwick, Birmingham.
BREL Derby	BREL, Derby Carriage Works (later ABB/Adtranz/ Bombardier Transportation Derby, now Alstom Derby).
Charles Roberts	Charles Roberts & Company, Horbury, Wakefield (later Bombardier Transportation).
Cravens	Cravens, Sheffield.
Derby	BR, Derby Carriage Works (later BREL Derby, then ABB/ Adtranz/Bombardier Transportation Derby, now Alstom Derby).
Doncaster	BR, Doncaster Works (later BREL Doncaster, then BRML Doncaster, then ABB/Adtranz Doncaster, then Bombardier).
Eastleigh	BR, Eastleigh Works (later BREL Eastleigh, then Wessex Traincare, and Alstom Eastleigh, now Arlington Fleet Services).
Glasgow	BR Springburn Works, Glasgow (now closed).

Gloucester	The Gloucester Railway Carriage & Wagon Co.
Hunslet-Barclay	Hunslet Barclay, Kilmarnock Works (later Wabtec Rail Scotland, now Brodies).
Metro-Cammell	Metropolitan-Cammell, Saltley, Birmingham (later GEC-Alsthom Birmingham, then Alstom Birmingham).
Pressed Steel	Pressed Steel, Linwood.
Swindon	BR Swindon Works.
Wolverton	BR Wolverton Works (later BREL Wolverton then Railcare, Wolverton, then Alstom, Wolverton now Gemini Rail Group).
York	BR, York Carriage Works (later BREL York, then ABB York).

Information on sub-contracting works which built parts of vehicles eg the underframes etc is not shown. In addition to the above, certain vintage Pullman cars were built or rebuilt at the following works:

Metropolitan Carriage & Wagon Company, Birmingham (later Alstom).
Midland Carriage & Wagon Company, Birmingham.
Pullman Car Company, Preston Park, Brighton.
Conversions have also been carried out at the Railway Technical Centre, Derby, LNWR, Crewe and Blakes Fabrications, Edinburgh.

ABBREVIATIONS

The following abbreviations are used in class headings and also throughout this publication:

BR	British Railways.
DB	Deutsche Bahn
DEMU	Diesel Electric Multiple Unit.
DMU	Diesel Multiple Unit (general term).
EMU	Electric Multiple Unit.
ETH	Electric Train Heating
ETS	Electric Train Supply
ft	feet
GWR	Great Western Railway
kN	kilonewtons.
km/h	kilometres per hour.
kW	kilowatts.
LT	London Transport.
LUL	London Underground Limited.
m	metres.
mph	miles per hour.
SR	BR Southern Region
t	tonnes

THE DEVELOPMENT OF BR STANDARD COACHES

Mark 1

The standard BR coach built from 1951 to 1963 was the Mark 1. This type features a separate underframe and body. The underframe is normally 64ft 6in long, but certain vehicles were built on shorter (57ft) frames. Tungsten lighting was standard and until 1961, BR Mark 1 bogies were generally provided. In 1959 Lot No. 30525 (Open Standard) appeared with fluorescent lighting and melamine interior panels, and from 1961 onwards Commonwealth bogies were fitted in an attempt to improve the quality of ride which became very poor when the tyre profiles on the wheels of the BR1 bogies became worn. Later batches of Open Standard and Open Brake Standard retained the features of Lot No. 30525, but compartment vehicles – whilst utilising melamine panelling in Standard Class – still retained tungsten lighting. Wooden interior finish was retained in First Class vehicles where the only change was to fluorescent lighting in open vehicles (except Lot No. 30648, which had tungsten lighting). In later years many Mark 1 coaches had BR 1 bogies replaced by B4. More recently a small number of carriages have had BR1 bogies replaced with Commonwealth bogies.

XP64

In 1964, a new prototype train was introduced. Known as "XP64", it featured new seat designs, pressure heating & ventilation, aluminium compartment doors and corridor partitions, foot pedal operated toilets and B4 bogies. The vehicles were built on standard Mark 1 underframes. Folding exterior doors were fitted, but these proved troublesome and were later replaced with hinged doors. All XP64 coaches have been withdrawn, but some have been preserved.

Mark 2

The prototype Mark 2 vehicle (W13252) was produced in 1963. This was a Corridor First of semi-integral construction and had pressure heating & ventilation, tungsten lighting, and was mounted on B4 bogies. This vehicle has now been preserved at the Mid Norfolk Railway. The production build was similar, but wider windows were used. The Open Standard vehicles used a new seat design similar to that in the XP64 and fluorescent lighting was provided. Interior finish reverted to wood. Mark 2 vehicles were built from 1964–66.

Mark 2A–2C

The Mark 2A design, built 1967–68, incorporated the remainder of the features first used in the XP64 coaches, ie foot pedal operated toilets (except Open Brake Standard), new First Class seat design, aluminium compartment doors and partitions together with fluorescent lighting in first class compartments. Folding gangway doors (lime green coloured) were used instead of the traditional one-piece variety.

Mark 2B coaches had wide wrap around doors at vehicle ends, no centre doors and a slightly longer body. In Standard Class there was one toilet at each end instead of two at one end as previously. The folding gangway doors were red.

Mark 2C coaches had a lowered ceiling with twin strips of fluorescent lighting and ducting for air conditioning, but air conditioning was never fitted.

Mark 2D–2F

These vehicles were fitted with air conditioning. They had no opening top-lights in saloon windows, which were shallower than previous ones.

Mark 2E vehicles had smaller toilets with luggage racks opposite. The folding gangway doors were fawn coloured.

Mark 2F vehicles had a modified air conditioning system, plastic interior panels and InterCity 70 type seats.

Mark 3

The Mark 3 design has BT10 bogies, is 75 ft (23 m) long and is of fully integral construction with InterCity 70 type seats. Gangway doors were yellow (red in Kitchen Buffet First) when new, although these were changed on refurbishment. Locomotive-hauled coaches are classified Mark 3A, Mark 3 being reserved for HST trailers. A new batch of Open First and Open Brake First, classified Mark 3B, was built in 1985 with Advanced Passenger Train-style seating and revised lighting. The last vehicles in the Mark 3 series were the driving brake vans ("Driving Van Trailers") built for West Coast Main Line services but now mostly withdrawn.

A number of Mark 3 vehicles were converted for use as HST trailers with CrossCountry, Grand Central and Great Western Railway.

Mark 4

The Mark 4 design was built by Metro-Cammell for use on the East Coast Main Line after electrification and featured a body profile suitable for tilting trains, although tilt is not fitted, and is not intended to be. This design is suitable for 140 mph running, although is restricted to 125 mph because the signalling system on the route is not suitable for the higher speed. The bogies for these coaches were built by SIG in Switzerland and are designated BT41. Power operated sliding plug exterior doors are standard. All Mark 4s were rebuilt with completely new interiors in 2003–05 for GNER and referred to as "Mallard" stock. These rakes generally run in fixed formations: eight are still operated by London North Eastern Railway and eight shorter sets by Transport for Wales.

New CAF carriages have recently been introduced by Caledonian Sleeper and TransPennine Express. CAF has designated them "Mark 5" and "Mark 5A" but it should be emphasised that these are not a development of the BR standard coach.

1. BRITISH RAILWAYS NUMBER SERIES COACHING STOCK

KITCHEN FIRST

Mark 1. Spent most of its life as a Royal Train vehicle and was numbered 2907 for a time. 24/–. B5 bogies. ETS 2.

Lot No. 30633 Swindon 1961. 41 t.

325	**VN**	WC	*WC*	CS	DUART

PULLMAN KITCHEN

Mark 2. Pressure Ventilated. Built with First Class seating but this has been replaced with a servery area. Gas cooking. 2T. B5 bogies. ETS 6.

Lot No. 30755 Derby 1966. 40 t.

504	**PC**	WC	*WC*	CS	ULLSWATER
506	**PC**	WC	*WC*	CS	WINDERMERE

PULLMAN OPEN FIRST

Mark 2. Pressure Ventilated. 36/– 2T. B4 bogies. ETS 5.

Lot No. 30754 Derby 1966. 35 t.

Non-standard livery: 546 Maroon & beige.

546	**O**	WC		CS	CITY OF MANCHESTER
548	**PC**	WC	*WC*	CS	GRASMERE
549	**PC**	WC	*WC*	CS	BASSENTHWAITE
550	**PC**	WC	*WC*	CS	RYDAL WATER
551	**PC**	WC	*WC*	CS	BUTTERMERE
552	**PC**	WC	*WC*	CS	ENNERDALE WATER
553	**PC**	WC	*WC*	CS	CRUMMOCK WATER

PULLMAN OPEN BRAKE FIRST

Mark 2. Pressure Ventilated. 30/– 2T. B4 bogies. ETS 4.

Lot No. 30753 Derby 1966. 35 t.

586	**PC**	WC	*WC*	CS	DERWENTWATER

BUFFET FIRST

Mark 2F. Air conditioned. Converted 1988–89/91 at BREL, Derby from Mark 2F Open Firsts. 1200/03/11/20/21 have Stones equipment, others have Temperature Ltd. 25/– 1T 1W. B4 bogies. d. ETS 6X.

1200/03/11/20. Lot No. 30845 Derby 1973. 33 t.
1207/10/12/21. Lot No. 30859 Derby 1973–74. 33 t.

1200	(3287, 6459)	**BG**	RV	*RV*	BU
1203	(3291)	**CC**	LS	*LS*	CL
1207	(3328, 6422) ·	**V**	WC		CS
1210	(3405, 6462)	**FS**	ER		YA
1211	(3305)	**PC**	LS	*LS*	CL	SNAEFELL
1212	(3427, 6453)	**BG**	RV	*RV*	BU
1220	(3315, 6432)	**FS**	ER		WO
1221	(3371)	**IC**	WC		CS

KITCHEN WITH BAR

Mark 1. Built with no seats but three Pullman-style seats now fitted in bar area. B5 bogies. ETS 1.

Lot No. 30624 Cravens 1960–61. 41 t.

1566	**VN**	WC	*WC*	CS	CAERDYDD

KITCHEN BUFFET UNCLASSIFIED

Mark 1. Built with 23 loose chairs. All remaining vehicles were refurbished with 23 fixed polypropylene chairs and fluorescent lighting. 1683/91 were further refurbished with 21 chairs, wheelchair space and carpets. ETS 2 (* 2X).

Now used on excursion trains with the seating area adapted to various uses including servery and food preparation areas, with some or all seating removed.

1651–91. Lot No. 30628 Pressed Steel 1960–61. Commonwealth bogies. 39 t.
1730. Lot No. 30512 BRCW 1960–61. B5 bogies. 37 t.

1651		**CH**	RV	*RV*	BU		1683		**RB**	RV		BU
1657		**BG**	RV	*RV*	BU		1691		**BG**	RV	*RV*	BU
1666	x	**M**	LS	*LS*	CL		1730	x	**CC**	SP	*SP*	BO
1671	x*	**BG**	RV	*RV*	BU							

BUFFET STANDARD

Mark 1. These carriages are basically an open standard with two full window spaces removed to accommodate a buffet counter, and four seats removed to allow for a stock cupboard. All remaining vehicles now have fluorescent lighting. –/44 2T. Commonwealth bogies. ETS 3.

1861 has had its toilets replaced with store cupboards.

1813–32. Lot No. 30520 Wolverton 1960. 38 t.
1840. Lot No. 30507 Wolverton 1960. 37 t.
1859–63. Lot No. 30670 Wolverton 1961–62. 38 t.
1882. Lot No. 30702 Wolverton 1962. 38 t.

1813	x	**CH**	RV	*RV*	BU		1860	x	**M**	WC	*WC*	CS
1832	x	**CH**	RV		BU		1861	x	**M**	WC	*WC*	CS
1840	v	**M**	WC	*WC*	CS		1863	x	**CC**	LS	*LS*	CL
1859	x	**M**	SP	*SP*	BO		1882	x	**M**	WC	*WC*	CS

KITCHEN UNCLASSIFIED

Mark 1. These carriages were built as Unclassified Restaurants. They were rebuilt with buffet counters and 23 fixed polypropylene chairs, then further refurbished by fitting fluorescent lighting. Further modified for use as servery vehicle with seating removed and kitchen extended. ETS 2X.

1953. Lot No. 30575 Swindon 1960. B4/B5 bogies. 36.5 t.
1961. Lot No. 30632 Swindon 1961. Commonwealth bogies. 39 t.

1953		**VN**	WC	*WC*	CS		1961	x	**M**	WC	*WC*	CS

HM THE QUEEN'S SALOON

Mark 3. Converted from an Open First built 1972. Consists of a lounge, bedroom and bathroom for HM The Queen, and a combined bedroom and bathroom for the Queen's dresser. One entrance vestibule has double doors. Air conditioned. BT10 bogies. ETS 9X.

Lot No. 30886 Wolverton 1977. 36 t.

2903	(11001)	**RP**	NR	*RT*		ZN

HRH THE DUKE OF EDINBURGH'S SALOON

Mark 3. Converted from an Open Standard built 1972. Consists of a combined lounge/dining room, a bedroom and a shower room for the Duke, a kitchen and a valet's bedroom and bathroom. Air conditioned. BT10 bogies. ETS 15X.

Lot No. 30887 Wolverton 1977. 36 t.

2904	(12001)	**RP**	NR	*RT*		ZN

ROYAL HOUSEHOLD SLEEPING CAR

Mark 3A. Built to similar specification as Sleeping Cars 10647–729. 12 sleeping compartments for use of Royal Household with a fixed lower berth and a hinged upper berth. 2T plus shower room. Air conditioned. BT10 bogies. ETS 11X.

Lot No. 31002 Derby/Wolverton 1985. 44 t.

| 2915 | | **RP** | NR | *RT* | ZN |

HRH THE PRINCE OF WALES'S DINING CAR

Mark 3. Converted from HST TRUK (kitchen car) built 1976. Large kitchen retained, but dining area modified for Royal use seating up to 14 at central table(s). Air conditioned. BT10 bogies. ETS 13X.

Lot No. 31059 Wolverton 1988. 43 t.

| 2916 | (40512) | **RP** | NR | *RT* | ZN |

ROYAL KITCHEN/HOUSEHOLD DINING CAR

Mark 3. Converted from HST TRUK built 1977. Large kitchen retained and dining area slightly modified with seating for 22 Royal Household members. Air conditioned. BT10 bogies. ETS 13X.

Lot No. 31084 Wolverton 1990. 43 t.

| 2917 | (40514) | **RP** | NR | *RT* | ZN |

ROYAL HOUSEHOLD CARS

Mark 3. Converted from HST TRUKs built 1976/77. Air conditioned. BT10 bogies. ETS 10X.

Lot Nos. 31083 (* 31085) Wolverton 1989. 41.05 t.

| 2918 | (40515) | **RP** | NR | | ZN |
| 2919 | (40518) * | **RP** | NR | | ZN |

ROYAL HOUSEHOLD COUCHETTES

Mark 2B. Converted from Corridor Brake First built 1969. Consists of luggage accommodation, guard's compartment, workshop area, 350 kW diesel generator and staff sleeping accommodation. B5 bogies. ETS 2X (when generator not in use). ETS index ?? (when generator in use).

Lot No. 31044 Wolverton 1986. 48 t.

| 2920 | (14109, 17109) | **RP** | NR | *RT* | ZN |

Mark 2B. Converted from Corridor Brake First built 1969. Consists of luggage accommodation, kitchen, brake control equipment and staff accommodation. B5 bogies. ETS 7X.

Lot No. 31086 Wolverton 1990. 41.5 t.

2921   (14107, 17107)   **RP**   NR   *RT*   ZN

HRH THE PRINCE OF WALES'S SLEEPING CAR

Mark 3B. Air conditioned. BT10 bogies. ETS 7X.

Lot No. 31035 Derby/Wolverton 1987.

2922   **RP**   NR   *RT*   ZN

ROYAL SALOON

Mark 3B. Air conditioned. BT10 bogies. ETS 6X.

Lot No. 31036 Derby/Wolverton 1987.

2923   **RP**   NR   *RT*   ZN

OPEN FIRST

Mark 1. 42/– 2T. ETS 3. Many now fitted with table lamps.

3058 was numbered DB 975313 and 3093 was numbered DB 977594 for a time when in departmental service for BR.

3045. Lot No. 30091 Doncaster 1954. B4 bogies. 33 t.
3058. Lot No. 30169 Doncaster 1955. Commonwealth bogies 35 t.
3091/93. Lot No. 30472 BRCW 1959. B4 bogies. 33 t.
3096–3100. Lot No. 30576 BRCW 1959. B4 bogies. 33 t.

3045	x **CC**	LS	*LS*	CL		3096	x **M**	SP	*SP*	BO
3058	x **M**	WC	*WC*	CS		3097	**CH**	WC		CS
3091	x **CH**	LS		ZG		3098	x **M**	WC	*WC*	CS
3093	x **M**	WC	*WC*	CS		3100	x **CC**	LS	*LS*	CL

Names:

3058	FLORENCE		3093	FLORENCE
3091	MARGUERITE			

Later design with fluorescent lighting, aluminium window frames and Commonwealth bogies.

3128/36/41/43/46/47/48 were renumbered 1058/60/63/65/68/69/70 when reclassified Restaurant Open First, then 3600/05/08/09/06/04/10 when declassified to Open Standard, but have since regained their original numbers. 3136 was numbered DB 977970 for a time when in use with Serco Railtest as a Brake Force Runner.

3105 has had its luggage racks removed and has tungsten lighting.

3105–28. Lot No. 30697 Swindon 1962–63. 36 t.
3130–50. Lot No. 30717 Swindon 1963. 36 t.

3105	x	**M**	WC	*WC*	CS		3125	x	**CC**	LS	*LS*	CL
3106	x	**M**	WC	*WC*	CS		3128	x	**M**	WC	*WC*	CS
3107	x	**CC**	LS	*LS*	CL		3130	x	**M**	WC	*WC*	CS
3110	x	**CH**	RV	*RV*	BU		3136	x	**M**	WC	*WC*	CS
3112	x	**CH**	SP		BO		3140	x	**CC**	LS		ZG
3113	x	**M**	WC	*WC*	CS		3141		**CH**	WC	*WC*	CS
3115	x	**M**	SP	*SP*	BO		3143	x	**M**	WC	*WC*	CS
3117	x	**M**	WC	*WC*	CS		3146		**CH**	WC		CS
3119	x	**CH**	WC		CS		3147		**CH**	WC		CS
3120		**M**	WC	*WC*	CS		3148		**CC**	LS	*LS*	CL
3121		**CH**	WC	*WC*	CS		3149		**CH**	WC	*WC*	CS
3122	x	**CC**	LS	*LS*	CL		3150		**CC**	SP	*SP*	BO
3123		**CH**	WC		CS							

Names:

3105	JULIA		3128	VICTORIA
3106	ALEXANDRA		3130	PAMELA
3113	JESSICA		3136	DIANA
3117	CHRISTINA		3143	PATRICIA

OPEN FIRST

Mark 2D. Air conditioned. Stones equipment. 42/– 2T. B4 bogies. ETS 5.

† Interior modified to Pullman Car standards with new seating, new panelling, tungsten lighting and table lights.

Lot No. 30821 Derby 1971–72. 34 t.

3174	†	**VN**	WC	*WC*	CS	GLAMIS
3182	†	**VN**	WC		CS	WARWICK
3188		**PC**	LS	*LS*	CL	CADAIR IDRIS

OPEN FIRST

Mark 2E. Air conditioned. Stones equipment. 42/– 2T (* 36/– 2T). B4 bogies. ETS 5.

r Refurbished with new seats.
† Interior modified to Pullman Car standards with new seating, new panelling, tungsten lighting and table lights.

Lot No. 30843 Derby 1972–73. 32.5 t. († 35.8 t).

3229		**PC**	LS	*LS*	CL	SNOWDON
3231	*	**PC**	LS	*LS*	CL	LOCHNAGAR
3232	dr	**BG**	WC		CS	
3247	†	**VN**	WC	*WC*	CS	CHATSWORTH
3267	†	**VN**	WC	*WC*	CS	BELVOIR
3273	†	**VN**	WC	*WC*	CS	ALNWICK
3275	†	**VN**	WC	*WC*	CS	HARLECH

OPEN FIRST

Mark 2F. Air conditioned. 3278–3314/3359–79 have Stones equipment, others have Temperature Ltd. All refurbished in the 1980s with power-operated vestibule doors, new panels and new seat trim. 42/– 2T. B4 bogies. d. ETS 5X.

r Further refurbished with table lamps and modified seats with burgundy seat trim.

3278–3314. Lot No. 30845 Derby 1973. 33.5 t.
3325–3426. Lot No. 30859 Derby 1973–74. 33.5 t.
3431–3438. Lot No. 30873 Derby 1974–75. 33.5 t.

3278	r	**BG**	RV	*RV*	BU	3356	r	**BG**	RV	*RV*	BU
3304	r	**BG**	RV	*RV*	BU	3359	r	**M**	WC	*WC*	CS
3312		**PC**	LS	*LS*	CL	3360	r	**PC**	WC	*WC*	CS
3313	r	**M**	WC	*WC*	CS	3362	r	**PC**	WC	*WC*	CS
3314	r	**BG**	RV	*RV*	BU	3364	r	**BG**	RV	*RV*	BU
3325	r	**BG**	RV	*RV*	BU	3384	r	**PC**	LS	*LS*	CL
3326	r	**M**	WC	*WC*	CS	3386	r	**BG**	RV	*RV*	BU
3330	r	**CC**	LS	*LS*	CL	3390	r	**BG**	RV	*RV*	BU
3333	r	**BG**	RV	*RV*	BU	3392	r	**M**	WC	*WC*	CS
3340	r	**BG**	RV	*RV*	BU	3395	r	**M**	WC	*WC*	CS
3344	r	**PC**	LS	*LS*	CL	3397	r	**BG**	RV	*RV*	BU
3345	r	**BG**	RV	*RV*	BU	3426	r	**PC**	LS	*LS*	CL
3348	r	**PC**	LS	*LS*	CL	3431	r	**M**	WC	*WC*	CS
3350	r	**M**	WC	*WC*	CS	3438	r	**PC**	LS	*LS*	CL
3352	r	**M**	WC	*WC*	CS						

Names:

3312	HELVELLYN	3384	PEN-Y-GHENT
3344	BEN CRUACHAN	3426	BEN NEVIS
3348	INGLEBOROUGH	3438	BEN LOMOND

OPEN STANDARD

Mark 1. –/64 2T. ETS 4.

4831–36. Lot No. 30506 Wolverton 1959. Commonwealth bogies. 37 t.
4854/56. Lot No. 30525 Wolverton 1959–60. B4 bogies. 33 t.

4831	x	**M**	SP	*SP*	BO	4854	x	**M**	WC	*WC*	CS
4832	x	**M**	SP	*SP*	BO	4856	x	**M**	SP	*SP*	BO
4836	x	**M**	SP	*SP*	BO						

OPEN STANDARD

Mark 1. Commonwealth bogies. –/64 2T. ETS 4.

4905. Lot No. 30646 Wolverton 1961. 36 t.
4927–5044. Lot No. 30690 Wolverton 1961–62. 37 t.

4905	x	**M**	WC	*WC*	CS	4984	x	**M**	WC	*WC*	CS
4927	x	**CC**	RV	*RV*	BU	4991		**CH**	WC		CS
4931	v	**M**	WC	*WC*	CS	4994	x	**M**	WC	*WC*	CS
4940	x	**M**	WC	*WC*	CS	4998		**CH**	WC		CS
4946	x	**CH**	RV	*RV*	BU	5009	x	**CH**	WC		CS
4949	x	**CH**	RV	*RV*	BU	5028	x	**M**	SP	*SP*	BO
4951	x	**M**	WC	*WC*	CS	5032	x	**M**	WC	*WC*	CS
4954	v	**M**	WC	*WC*	CS	5033	x	**M**	WC	*WC*	CS
4959		**CH**	WC		CS	5035	x	**M**	WC	*WC*	CS
4960	x	**M**	WC	*WC*	CS	5044	x	**M**	WC	*WC*	CS
4973	x	**M**	WC	*WC*	CS						

OPEN STANDARD

Mark 2. Pressure ventilated. –/64 2T. B4 bogies. ETS 4.

Lot No. 30751 Derby 1965–67. 32 t.

5157	v	**CH**	VT	*VT*	TM	5200	v	**M**	WC	*WC*	CS
5171	v	**M**	WC	*WC*	CS	5212	v	**CH**	VT	*VT*	TM
5177	v	**CH**	VT	*VT*	TM	5216	v	**M**	WC	*WC*	CS
5191	v	**CH**	VT	*VT*	TM	5222	v	**M**	WC	*WC*	CS
5198	v	**CH**	VT	*VT*	TM						

OPEN STANDARD

Mark 2. Pressure ventilated. –/48 2T. B4 bogies. ETS 4.

Lot No. 30752 Derby 1966. 32 t.

5229		**M**	WC	*WC*	CS	5239		**M**	WC	*WC*	CS
5236	v	**M**	WC	*WC*	CS	5249	v	**M**	WC	*WC*	CS
5237	v	**M**	WC	*WC*	CS						

Name: 5239 LEIGH

OPEN STANDARD

Mark 2A. Pressure ventilated. –/64 2T (w –/62 2T). B4 bogies. ETS 4.

f Facelifted vehicles.

5278–92. Lot No. 30776 Derby 1967–68. 32 t.
5366–5419. Lot No. 30787 Derby 1968. 32 t.

5278		**M**	WC	*WC*	CS	5366	f	**CC**	LS	*LS*	CL
5292	f	**CC**	RV		BU	5419	w	**M**	WC	*WC*	CS

OPEN STANDARD

Mark 2B. Pressure ventilated. –/62. B4 bogies. ETS 4.

Lot No. 30791 Derby 1969. 32 t.

| 5453 | | **M** | WC | *WC* | CS | | 5487 | | **M** | WC | *WC* | CS |

OPEN STANDARD

Mark 2E. Air conditioned. Stones equipment. Refurbished with new interior panelling. –/64 2T. B4 bogies. d. ETS 5.

s   Modified design of seat headrest and centre luggage stack. –/60 2T.

5787. Lot No. 30837 Derby 1972. 33.5 t.
5810. Lot No. 30844 Derby 1972–73. 33.5 t.

| 5787 | s | **DS** ER | YA | | 5810 | | **DR** ER | YA |

OPEN STANDARD

Mark 2F. Air conditioned. Temperature Ltd equipment. InterCity 70 seats. All were refurbished in the 1980s with power-operated vestibule doors, new panels and seat trim. They have subsequently undergone a second refurbishment with carpets and new seat trim. Carriages used as Network Rail Service Stock can be found in the Service Stock section. –/64 2T. B4 bogies. d. ETS 5X.

q   Fitted with two wheelchair spaces. –/60 2T 2W.
s   Fitted with centre luggage stack. –/60 2T.
t   Fitted with centre luggage stack and wheelchair space. –/58 2T 1W.

5912–55. Lot No. 30846 Derby 1973. 33 t.
5961–6158. Lot No. 30860 Derby 1973–74. 33 t.
6173–83. Lot No. 30874 Derby 1974–75. 33 t.

5912		**PC**	LS	*LS*	CL		5998		**BG**	RV	*RV*	BU
5919	pt	**DR**	ER		YA		6000	t	**M**	WC	*WC*	CS
5921		**AR**	RV	*RV*	BU		6008	s	**DS**	NR		CF
5929		**BG**	RV	*RV*	BU		6012		**M**	WC	*WC*	CS
5937		**DS**	ER		YA		6021		**PC**	WC	*WC*	CS
5945		**SR**	RV		BU		6022	s	**M**	WC	*WC*	CS
5950		**AR**	RV	*RV*	BU		6024		**BG**	RV	*RV*	BU
5952		**BG**	RV	*RV*	BU		6027	q	**SR**	RV		BU
5955		**SR**	RV		BU		6042		**AR**	RV	*RV*	BU
5961	pt	**BG**	RV	*RV*	BU		6046		**DR**	ER		YA
5964		**AR**	RV	*RV*	BU		6051		**BG**	RV	*RV*	BU
5965	t	**SR**	RV		BU		6054		**BG**	RV	*RV*	BU
5976	t	**SR**	RV		BU		6064		**DS**	ER		YA
5985		**AR**	RV	*RV*	BU		6067	pt	**BG**	RV	*RV*	BU
5987		**SR**	RV		BU		6103		**M**	WC	*WC*	CS
5991		**CC**	LS	*LS*	CL		6115	s	**M**	WC	*WC*	CS

6137	s pt	**SR**	RV		BU		6176	t	**BG**	RV	RV	BU
6158		**BG**	RV	RV	BU		6177	s	**SR**	RV		BU
6173		**DS**	ER		YA		6183	s	**SR**	RV		BU

BRAKE GENERATOR VAN

Mark 1. Renumbered 1989 from BR departmental series. Converted from Gangwayed Brake Van in 1973 to three-phase supply brake generator van for use with HST trailers. Modified 1999 for use with locomotive-hauled stock. B5 bogies. ETS index ??.

Lot No. 30400 Pressed Steel 1958.

6310	(81448, 975325)	**CH**	RV	RV		BU

GENERATOR VAN

Mark 1. Converted from Gangwayed Brake Vans in 1992. B4 (* B5) bogies. ETS index 75.

6311. Lot No. 30162 Pressed Steel 1958. 37.25 t.
6312. Lot No. 30224 Cravens 1956. 37.25 t.
6313. Lot No. 30484 Pressed Steel 1958. 37.25 t.

6311	(80903, 92911)		**CC**	LS	LS	CL
6312	(81023, 92925)		**M**	WC	WC	CS
6313	(81553, 92167)	*	**PC**	BE	BP	SL

BUFFET STANDARD

Mark 2C. Converted from Open Standard by removal of one seating bay and replacing this with a counter with a space for a trolley, now replaced with a more substantial buffet. Adjacent toilet removed and converted to steward's washing area/store. Pressure ventilated. –/55 1T. B4 bogies. ETS 4.

Lot No. 30795 Derby 1969–70. 32.5 t.

6528	(5592)		**M**	WC	WC	CS

SLEEPER RECEPTION CAR

Mark 2F. Converted from Open First. These vehicles consist of pantry, microwave cooking facilities, seating area for passengers (with loose chairs, staff toilet plus two bars). Later refurbished again with new "sofa" seating as well as the loose chairs. Converted at RTC, Derby (6700), Ilford (6701–05) and Derby (6706–08). Air conditioned.

6700/01/03/05–08 have Stones equipment and 6702/04 have Temperature Ltd equipment. The number of seats per coach can vary but typically is 25/–1T (12 seats as "sofa" seating and 13 loose chairs). B4 bogies. d. ETS 5X.

6705 and 6706 have been rebuilt as private saloons. Full details awaited.

6708 also carries the branding "THE HIPPOCRENE BAR".

6700–02/04/08. Lot No. 30859 Derby 1973–74. 33.5 t.
6703/05–07. Lot No. 30845 Derby 1973. 33.5 t.

6700	(3347)	**CA**	ER		YA	
6701	(3346)	**CA**	BR		ZK	
6702	(3421)	**FS**	ER		YA	
6703	(3308)	**CA**	ER		WO	
6704	(3341)	**FS**	ER		YA	
6705	(3310, 6430)	**CC**	LS	*LS*	CL	ARDNAMURCHAN
6706	(3283, 6421)	**CC**	LS	*LS*	CL	MOUNT MGAHINGA
6707	(3276, 6418)	**FS**	ER		YA	
6708	(3370)	**PC**	LS	*LS*	CL	MOUNT HELICON

BUFFET FIRST

Mark 2D. Converted from Buffet Standard by the removal of another seating bay and fitting a more substantial buffet counter with boiler and microwave oven. Now converted to First Class with new seating and end luggage stacks. Air conditioned. Stones equipment. 30/– 1T. B4 bogies. d. ETS 5. Lot No. 30822 Derby 1971. 33 t.

6723	(5641, 6662)	**M**	WC		CS	
6724	(5721, 6665)	**M**	WC	*WC*	CS	

OPEN BRAKE STANDARD WITH TROLLEY SPACE

Mark 2. This vehicle uses the same bodyshell as Mark 2 Corridor Brake Firsts and has First Class seat spacing and wider tables. Converted from Open Brake Standard by removal of one seating bay and replacing this with a counter with a space for a trolley. Adjacent toilet removed and converted to a steward's washing area/store. –/23. B4 bogies. ETS 4.

Lot No. 30757 Derby 1966. 31 t.

9101	(9398)	v	**CH**	VT	*VT*	TM	

▲ BR chocolate & cream-liveried Mark 1 Kitchen Buffet Unclassified 1651 is seen at Banbury on 29/10/22. **Mark Beal**

▼ BR blue & grey-liveried Mark 1 Kitchen Buffet Unclassified 1657 is seen at Paddock Wood on 11/06/23. **Robert Pritchard**

▲ Royal Train-liveried Mark 2B Royal Household Couchette 2920 is seen near Milton Keynes on 08/06/23. **Mark Beal**

▼ BR carmine & cream-liveried Mark 1 Open First 3045 is seen at Girvan on 21/09/22. **Andy Chard**

▲ BR maroon-liveried Mark 2F Open First 3326 is seen at Wandel on 14.06.23.
Robin Ralston

▼ BR blue & grey-liveried Mark 2F Open First 3397 is seen at Maidstone East on 11/06/23.
Robert Pritchard

▲ Pullman Car Company-liveried Mark 2F Open First 3426 "Ben Nevis" is seen at Penzance on 05/08/23. **Ian Beardsley**

▼ BR carmine & cream-liveried Mark 1 Open Standard 4927 is seen at Banbury on 29/10/22. **Mark Beal**

▲ BR chocolate & cream-liveried Mark 2 Open Standard 5191 is seen at Totnes on 24/08/22. **Robin Ralston**

▼ Pullman Car Company-liveried VSOE Generator Van 6313 is seen at Crofton Park on 09/04/23. **Robert Pritchard**

▲ BR carmine & cream-liveried former Sleeper Reception Car 6705 has been rebuilt as a private saloon for Locomotive Services. It is seen at Woofferton (near Ludlow) on 07/04/23. **Dave Gommersall**

▼ ScotRail InterCity-liveried Driving Open Brake Standard 9707 is seen near Linlithgow with the 09.02 Edinburgh–Glasgow Queen Street railtour on 25/02/23, being propelled by 47712. **Richard Birse**

▲ Still in Greater Anglia livery, with "The Real Charter Train Co." branding, is Mark 3B Open First 11099, seen near Mexborough on 19/03/23. **Robert Pritchard**

▼ New LNER oxblood-liveried Mark 4 Open First (Disabled) 11318 is seen at London King's Cross on 12/08/23. **Ian Beardsley**

▲ ScotRail InterCity-liveried Mark 3A Open Standard 12171 is seen at Keighley on the Keighley & Worth Valley Railway on 25/05/23. **Robert Pritchard**

▼ Transport for Wales black-liveried Mark 4 Open Standard (End) 12211 (previously in Grand Central livery) is seen at Cardiff Central on 14/04/23. **Robert Pritchard**

▲ Chiltern Railways Mainline-liveried Mark 3A Open Standard 12615 is seen at Beaconsfield on 09/04/22.　　　**Robert Pritchard**

▼ TransPennine Express-liveried Mark 5A Driving Open Brake Standard 12814 leads the 09.26 Cleethorpes–Manchester Airport away from Sheffield on 09/12/22.　　　**Robert Pritchard**

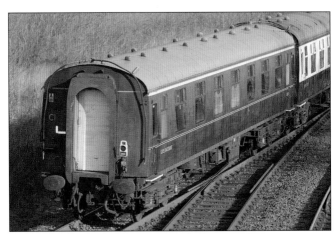

▲ BR maroon-liveried Mark 1 Open First 13230 is seen at Inverkeithing East Junction on 01/02/23. **Robin Ralston**

▼ Caledonian Sleeper-liveried Sleeper Seated Carriage with brake 15005 is seen at Ravenstruther on 30/12/22. **Robin Ralston**

▲ BR blue & grey-liveried Mark 2B Couchette/Generator Coach 17105 is seen at Paddock Wood on 11/06/23. **Robert Pritchard**

▼ BR maroon-liveried Mark 1 Corridor Brake Standard support carriage 35486 is seen at London King's Cross on 16/10/22. **Robert Pritchard**

▲ BR InterCity-liveried Mark 3B Driving Brake Van 82139 leads the 14.29 Crewe–London Euston away from Crewe on 19/08/21. **Cliff Beeton**

▼ In a special livery for the Alzheimer's Society Cymru, Transport for Wales Mark 4 Driving Brake Van 82226 brings up the rear of the 06.27 Manchester Piccadilly–Cardiff Central at Newport on 19/06/23. **Robert Pritchard**

▲ Midland Pullman-liveried HST Trailer Kitchen Buffet First 40802 is seen near Drem on 03/04/23. **Robin Ralston**

▼ ScotRail InterCity-liveried HST Trailer Standard 42300 is seen at Bishopbriggs on 09/06/23. **Robert Pritchard**

▲ Great Western Railway-liveried HST Trailer Guard's Standard 49109 is seen at Par on 06/06/23. **Robert Pritchard**

▼ Royal Scotsman State Car No. 4 (Saloon 99964) is seen near Breich on the Shotts line on 27/03/23. **Robin Ralston**

▲ BR carmine & cream-liveried Club Car 99993 is seen at Woofferton (near Ludlow) on 07/04/23. **Dave Gommersall**

▼ Pullman Car Company-liveried VSOE Pullman Kitchen First 284 "VERA" is seen at Crofton Park on 09/04/23. **Robert Pritchard**

▲ Network Rail yellow-liveried Mark 2B Test Train Staff Coach 977969 is seen near Saxilby on 12/11/22. **Robert Pritchard**

▼ Network Rail yellow-liveried New Measurement Train Staff Coach 977984 is seen at Mexborough on 19/03/23. **Robert Pritchard**

OPEN BRAKE STANDARD

Mark 2. These vehicles use the same bodyshell as Mark 2 Corridor Brake Firsts and have First Class seat spacing and wider tables. Pressure ventilated. –/31 1T. B4 bogies. ETS 4.

9104 was originally numbered 9401. It was renumbered when converted to Open Brake Standard with trolley space. Now returned to original layout.

Lot No. 30757 Derby 1966. 31.5 t.

9104	v	**M**	WC	WC	CS		9392	v	**M**	WC	WC	CS
9391		**M**	WC	WC	CS							

OPEN BRAKE STANDARD

Mark 2D. Air conditioned. Stones Equipment. B4 bogies. d. pg. ETS 5.

r Refurbished with new interior panelling –/31 1T.
s Refurbished with new seating –/22 1TD.

Lot No. 30824 Derby 1971. 33 t.

9479	r	**PC**	LS	LS	CL		9493	s	**M**	WC	WC	CS
9488	s	**SR**	DR		ML							

OPEN BRAKE STANDARD

Mark 2E. Air conditioned. Stones Equipment. Refurbished with new interior panelling. –/32 1T (* –/30 1T 1W). B4 bogies. d. pg. ETS 5.

Lot No. 30838 Derby 1972. 33 t.

Non-standard livery: 9502 Pullman umber & cream.

s Modified design of seat headrest.

9497		**CA**	ER		WO		9507	s	**BG**	RV	RV	BU
9502	s	**0**	BE	BP	SL		9509	s	**AV**	RV		BU
9504	s*	**BG**	RV	RV	BU							

OPEN BRAKE STANDARD

Mark 2F. Air conditioned. Temperature Ltd equipment. All were refurbished in the 1980s with power-operated vestibule doors, new panels and seat trim. All now further refurbished with carpets. –/32 1T (w –/30 1T 1W). B4 bogies. d. pg. ETS 5X.

9537 has had all its seats removed for the purpose of carrying luggage.

Lot No. 30861 Derby 1974. 34 t.

9513		**IC**	ER		CL		9526	n	**BG**	RV	RV	BU
9520	nw	**AR**	RV	RV	BU		9527	n	**SR**	RV		BU
9521		**DS**	RV		BU		9537	n	**V**	RV		BU
9525		**DR**	LO		CN		9539		**SR**	RV		BU

DRIVING OPEN BRAKE STANDARD

Mark 2F. Air conditioned. Temperature Ltd equipment. Push & pull (tdm system). Converted from Open Brake Standard, these vehicles originally had high cabs at the brake end. They have since been refurbished and have had their cabs widened and the cab-end gangways removed. Five vehicles (9701–03/08/14) have been converted for use in Network Rail test trains and can be found in the Service Stock section of this book. –/30(+1) 1W. B4 bogies. d. pg. Cowcatchers. ETS 5X.

Lot No. 30861 Derby 1974. Converted Glasgow 1979. Disc brakes. 34 t.

9704	(9512)	**DS**	LS		CL	9709	(9515)	**DS**	ER		YA
9705	(9519)	**DS**	ER		YA	9710	(9518)	**DS**	ER		YA
9707	(9511)	**IS**	LS		CL						

OPEN BRAKE UNCLASSIFIED

Mark 2E. Converted from Open Standard with new seating by Railcare, Wolverton. Air conditioned. Stones equipment. Five vehicles (9801/03/06/08/10) are currently used in Network Rail test trains and can be found in the Service Stock section of this book. –/31 2T. B4 bogies. d. ETS 4X.

9800/02. Lot No. 30837 Derby 1972. 33.5 t.
9804–09. Lot No. 30844 Derby 1972–73. 33.5 t.

9800	(5751)	**CA**	ER		WO	9805	(5833)	**FS**	ER		YA
9802	(5772)	**CA**	ER		YA	9807	(5851)	**FS**	ER		YA
9804	(5826)	**FS**	LS		CL	9809	(5890)	**FS**	ER		YA

KITCHEN BUFFET FIRST

Mark 3A. Air conditioned. Converted from HST catering vehicles and Mark 3 Open Firsts. 18/– plus two seats for staff use (* 24/–, † 35/– 1T, t 23/– 1T 1W). BT10 bogies. d. ETS 14X.

† Refurbished Great Western Railway Sleeper coaches fitted with new Transcal seating.

Non-standard liveries:

10211 EWS dark maroon.
10241 Livery trials.

10211. Lot No. 30884 Derby 1977. 39.8 t.
10212–229. Lot No. 30878 Derby 1975–76. 39.8 t.
10237–259. Lot No. 30890 Derby 1979. 39.8 t.

10211	(40510)		**O**	DB	*DB*	TO	10229	(11059)	*	**GA**	ER		WO
10212	(11049)		**VT**	ER		YA	10237	(10022)	*	**B**	NS		BU
10217	(11051)	†	**GW**	P	*GW*	PZ	10241	(10009)	*	**O**	P		IL
10219	(11047)	†	**GW**	P	*GW*	PZ	10249	(10012)	t	**AW**	ER		YA
10225	(11014)	†	**GW**	P	*GW*	PZ	10259	(10025)	t	**AW**	ER		YA

KITCHEN BUFFET FIRST

Mark 3A. Air conditioned. Rebuilt 2011–12 and fitted with sliding plug doors. Interiors originally refurbished for Wrexham & Shropshire with Primarius seating, a new kitchen area and universal-access toilet. Retention toilets. 30/– 1TD 1W. BT10 bogies. ETS 14X.

10271/273/274. Lot No. 30890 Derby 1979. 41.3 t.
10272. Lot No. 30884 Derby 1977. 41.3 t.

10271 (10018, 10236)	**CM**	AV	*CR*	AL
10272 (40517, 10208)	**CM**	AV	*CR*	AL
10273 (10021, 10230)	**CM**	AV	*CR*	AL
10274 (10010, 10255)	**CM**	AV	*CR*	AL

KITCHEN BUFFET STANDARD

Mark 4. Air conditioned. Rebuilt from First to Standard Class with bar adjacent to seating area instead of adjacent to end of coach. Retention toilets. –/30 1T. BT41 bogies. ETS 6X.

Lot No. 31045 Metro-Cammell 1989–92. 43.2 t.

10300	**LC**	E	*LN*	NL	10315	**LC**	E	*LN*	NL
10301	**TB**	TW	*TW*	CP	10318	**TB**	TW	*TW*	CP
10305	**VE**	TW		BK	10321	**TB**	TW	*TW*	CP
10306	**LC**	E	*LN*	NL	10324	**LC**	E	*LN*	NL
10309	**LC**	E	*LN*	NL	10325	**VE**	TW	*TW*	CP
10311	**LC**	E	*LN*	NL	10328	**VE**	TW	*TW*	CP
10312	**VE**	TW	*TW*	CP	10330	**TB**	TW	*TW*	CP
10313	**LC**	E	*LN*	NL	10333	**LC**	E	*LN*	NL

BUFFET STANDARD or FIRST

Mark 3A. Air conditioned. Converted from Mark 3 Open Standard at Derby 2006. –/54 * now fitted with First Class seating. 32/–. d. ETS 13X.

Lot No. 30877 Derby 1975–77. 37.8 t.

10404 (12068)	* **IS**	LS	*LS*	CL
10406 (12020)	**GA**	TL	*RA*	GA

BUFFET STANDARD

Mark 3A. Air conditioned. Converted from Mark 3 Kitchen Buffet First 2015–16. –/54. BT10 bogies. d. ETS 13X.

10411. Lot No. 30884 Derby 1977. 37.8 t.
10413/416. Lot No. 30878 Derby 1975–76. 37.8 t.
10417. Lot No. 30890 Derby 1979. 37.8 t.

10411	(40519, 10200)	**IC**	LS	*LS*	CL
10413	(11034, 10214)	**GA**	ER		YA
10416	(11035, 10228)	**IC**	LS	*LS*	CL

SLEEPING CAR WITH PANTRY

Mark 3A. Air conditioned. Retention toilets. 12 compartments with a fixed lower berth and a hinged upper berth, plus an attendant's compartment (* 11 compartments with a fixed lower berth and a hinged upper berth + one compartment for a disabled person. 1TD). 2T. BT10 bogies. d. ETS 7X.

Non-standard livery: 10546 EWS dark maroon.

Lot No. 30960 Derby 1981–83. 41 t.

10501	**FS**	ER		YA	10584		**GW**	P	*GW*	PZ
10502	**FS**	ER		YA	10589		**GW**	P	*GW*	PZ
10504	**FS**	LS		KR	10590		**GW**	P	*GW*	PZ
10513	**FS**	LS		KR	10594		**GW**	P	*GW*	PZ
10519	**CC**	LS	*LS*	CL	10596		**GW**	P	*GW*	PZ
10520	**CC**	LS	*LS*	CL	10600		**FS**	ER		YA
10532	**GW**	P	*GW*	PZ	10601	*	**GW**	P	*GW*	PZ
10534	**GW**	P	*GW*	PZ	10610		**FS**	WC		CS
10546	**0**	DB	*DB*	TO	10612	*	**GW**	P	*GW*	PZ
10551	**FS**	P		LA	10614		**FS**	WC		CS
10553	**FS**	P		LA	10616	*	**GW**	P	*GW*	PZ
10563	**GW**	P	*GW*	PZ						

SLEEPING CAR

Mark 3A. Air conditioned. Retention toilets. 13 compartments with a fixed lower berth and a hinged upper berth (* 11 compartments with a fixed lower berth and a hinged upper berth + one compartment for a disabled person. 1TD). 2T. BT10 bogies. ETS 6X.

10734 was originally 2914 and used as a Royal Train staff sleeping car. It has 12 berths and a shower room and is ETS 11X.

10648–729. Lot No. 30961 Derby 1980–84. 43.5 t.
10734. Lot No. 31002 Derby/Wolverton 1985. 42.5 t.

10648	d*	**FS**	LS		KR	10703	d	**VN**	WC	*WC*	CS
10650	d*	**FS**	LS		KR	10714	d*	**FS**	PO		CS
10675	d	**FS**	LS		KR	10718	d*	**FS**	WC		CS
10683	d	**FS**	LS		KR	10719	d*	**FS**	PO		CS
10688	d	**PC**	LS	*LS*	CL	10729		**VN**	WC	*WC*	CS
10699	d*	**FS**	ER		YA	10734		**VN**	WC	*WC*	CS

Names:

| 10729 | CREWE | | 10734 | BALMORAL |

OPEN FIRST

Mark 3A. Air conditioned. All refurbished with table lamps and new seat cushions and trim. 48/– 2T. BT10 bogies. d. ETS 6X.

Non-standard livery: 11039 EWS dark maroon.

Lot No. 30878 Derby 1975–76. 34.3 t.

11018	**VT**	ER		YA	11048	**VT**	ER	YA
11039	**O**	DB	*DB*	TO				

OPEN FIRST

Mark 3B. Air conditioned. InterCity 80 seats. All refurbished with table lamps and new seat cushions and trim. Retention toilets. 48/– 1T. BT10 bogies. d. ETS 6X.

† Fitted with disabled toilet and reduced seating, including three Compin Pegasus seats. 37/– 1TD 2W.

Non-standard livery: 11074 Original HST prototype grey & BR blue.

Lot No. 30982 Derby 1985. 36.5 t.

11066		**IS**	LS	*LS*	CL	11087 †	**IC**	LS	*LS*	CL
11068		**IC**	LS	*LS*	CL	11090 †	**GA**	ER		YA
11070		**IC**	LS	*LS*	CL	11091		**IC**	LS	*LS*	CL
11074		**O**	ER		YA	11092 †	**GA**	TL	*RA*	GA
11075		**IC**	LS	*LS*	CL	11093 †	**GA**	TL	*RA*	GA
11076		**IC**	LS	*LS*	CL	11095 †	**GA**	ER		YA
11077		**IC**	LS	*LS*	CL	11098 †	**IC**	LS	*LS*	CL
11078 †	**GA**	ER		YA	11099 †	**GA**	TL	*RA*	GA
11082		**IS**	LS	*LS*	CL	11101 †	**GA**	TL	*RA*	GA

OPEN FIRST

Mark 4. Air conditioned. Rebuilt with new interior by Bombardier Wakefield 2003–05 (some converted from Standard Class vehicles). Retention toilets. 41/– 1T (plus 2 seats for staff use). BT41 bogies. ETS 6X.

11229. Lot No. 31046 Metro-Cammell 1989–92. 41.3 t.
11279–295. Lot No. 31049 Metro-Cammell 1989–92. 41.3 t.

11229		**LC**	E	*LN*	NL	11286 (12482)	**LC**	E	*LN*	NL
11279 (12521)	**LC**	E	*LN*	NL	11288 (12517)	**LC**	E	*LN*	NL
11284 (12487)	**LC**	E	*LN*	NL	11295 (12475)	**LC**	E	*LN*	NL
11285 (12537)	**LC**	E	*LN*	NL					

OPEN FIRST (DISABLED)

Mark 4. Air conditioned. Rebuilt from Open First by Bombardier Wakefield 2003–05. Retention toilets. 42/– 1TD 1W. BT41 bogies. ETS 6X.

Lot No. 31046 Metro-Cammell 1989–92. 40.7 t.

11306	(11276)	**LC**	E	*LN*	NL	11319	(11247)	**TB**	TW	*TW* CP
11308	(11263)	**LC**	E	*LN*	NL	11320	(11255)	**TB**	TW	*TW* CP
11312	(11225)	**LC**	E	*LN*	NL	11321	(11245)	**TB**	TW	*TW* CP
11313	(11210)	**LC**	E	*LN*	NL	11322	(11228)	**TB**	TW	*TW* CP
11315	(11238)	**LC**	E	*LN*	NL	11323	(11235)	**VE**	TW	*TW* CP
11316	(11227)	**VE**	TW		BK	11324	(11253)	**VE**	TW	*TW* CP
11317	(11223)	**LC**	E	*LN*	NL	11325	(11231)	**VE**	TW	*TW* CP
11318	(11251)	**LC**	E	*LN*	NL	11326	(11206)	**LC**	E	*LN* NL

OPEN FIRST

Mark 4. Air conditioned. Rebuilt from Open First by Bombardier Wakefield 2003–05. Separate area for 7 smokers, although smoking is no longer allowed. Retention toilets. 46/– 1TD 1W. BT41 bogies. ETS 6X.

Lot No. 31046 Metro-Cammell 1989–92. 42.1 t.

11406	(11205)	**LC**	E	*LN*	NL	11416	(11254)	**LC**	E	*LN* NL
11408	(11218)	**LC**	E	*LN*	NL	11417	(11226)	**LC**	E	*LN* NL
11412	(11209)	**LC**	E	*LN*	NL	11418	(11222)	**LC**	E	*LN* NL
11413	(11212)	**LC**	E	*LN*	NL	11426	(11252)	**LC**	E	*LN* NL
11415	(11208)	**LC**	E	*LN*	NL					

OPEN FIRST

CAF Mark 5A. Air conditioned. TransPennine Express coaches. Retention toilets. 30/– 1TD 2W. CAF bogies. ETS XX.

CAF Beasain 2017–18. 32.7 t.

11501	**TP**	BN	*TP*	MA	11508	**TP**	BN	*TP*	MA
11502	**TP**	BN	*TP*	MA	11509	**TP**	BN	*TP*	MA
11503	**TP**	BN	*TP*	MA	11510	**TP**	BN	*TP*	MA
11504	**TP**	BN	*TP*	MA	11511	**TP**	BN	*TP*	MA
11505	**TP**	BN	*TP*	MA	11512	**TP**	BN	*TP*	MA
11506	**TP**	BN	*TP*	MA	11513	**TP**	BN	*TP*	MA
11507	**TP**	BN	*TP*	MA					

OPEN STANDARD

Mark 3A. Air conditioned. All refurbished with modified seat backs and new layout and further refurbished with new seat trim. –/76 2T († –/70 2T 1W, z –/70 1TD 1T 2W). BT10 bogies. d. ETS 6X.

* Further refurbished with more unidirectional seating and one toilet removed. Retention toilets. –/80 1T (t –/64 1T).
s Refurbished Sleeper day coaches fitted with new Transcal seating to a 2+2 layout and a universal access toilet. Retention toilets. –/65 1TD 1W.

12171 was converted from Open Composite 11910, formerly Open First 11010.

Non-standard livery: 12092 Original HST prototype grey & BR blue.

12021–167. Lot No. 30877 Derby 1975–77. 34.3 t.
12171. Lot No. 30878 Derby 1975–76. 34.3 t.

12021	*	**GA**	ER		YA	12100	s	**GW**	P	*GW*	PZ
12032	*	**GA**	ER		YA	12111	*t	**IS**	LS	*LS*	CL
12036	†	**CM**	ER		YA	12122	z	**VT**	ER		YA
12043	†	**CM**	ER		YA	12125	*	**GA**	TL	*RA*	GA
12061	*	**GA**	NS		BU	12133		**VT**	ER		YA
12064	*	**GA**	ER		YA	12137	*	**GA**	NS		BU
12078		**VT**	ER		YA	12138		**VT**	ER		YA
12079	*	**GA**	NS		BU	12142	s	**GW**	P	*GW*	PZ
12090	*	**GA**	NS		BU	12146	*	**GA**	NS		BU
12091	*	**GA**	ER		YA	12154	*	**GA**	TL	*RA*	GA
12092		**O**	ER		YA	12161	s	**GW**	P	*GW*	PZ
12094		**CM**	ER		YA	12164	*	**GA**	NS		BU
12097	*	**GA**	ER		YA	12167	*	**GA**	NS		BU
12098	*	**GA**	ER		YA	12171	*t	**IS**	LS	*LS*	CL

OPEN STANDARD

Mark 3A (†) or Mark 3B. Air conditioned. Converted from Mark 3A or 3B Open First. Fitted with Grammer seating. –/70 2T 1W. BT10 bogies. d. ETS 6X.

12176/180. Mark 3B. Lot No. 30982 Derby 1985. 38.5 t.
12182. Mark 3A. Lot No. 30878 Derby 1975–76. 38.5 t.

12176	(11064)		**AW**	ER	YA
12180	(11084)		**AW**	ER	YA
12182	(11013)	†	**AW**	ER	YA

OPEN STANDARD (END)

Mark 4. Air conditioned. Rebuilt with new interior by Bombardier Wakefield 2003–05. Separate area for 26 smokers, although smoking is no longer allowed. Retention toilets. –/76 1T. BT41 bogies. ETS 6X.

Lot No. 31047 Metro-Cammell 1989–91. 39.5 t.

12205	**LC**	E	*LN*	NL	12219	**VE**	TW	*TW*	CP
12208	**LC**	E	*LN*	NL	12220	**LC**	E	*LN*	NL
12210	**TB**	TW	*TW*	CP	12222	**TB**	TW	*TW*	CP
12211	**TB**	TW	*TW*	CP	12223	**LC**	E	*LN*	NL
12212	**LC**	E	*LN*	NL	12224	**TB**	TW	*TW*	CP
12213	**LC**	E	*LN*	NL	12225	**VE**	TW	*TW*	CP
12214	**LC**	E	*LN*	NL	12226	**LC**	E	*LN*	NL
12215	**VE**	TW		LE	12228	**LC**	E	*LN*	NL
12217	**VE**	TW	*TW*	CP					

OPEN STANDARD (DISABLED)

Mark 4. Air conditioned. Rebuilt with new interior by Bombardier Wakefield 2003–05. Retention toilets. –/68 2W 1TD. BT41 bogies. ETS 6X.

Lot No. 31048 Metro-Cammell 1989–91. 39.4 t.

12303	**LC**	E	*LN*	NL	12315	**VE**	TW	*TW*	CP
12304	**VE**	TW	*TW*	CP	12316	**TB**	TW	*TW*	CP
12308	**VE**	TW		BK	12323	**TB**	TW	*TW*	CP
12309	**LC**	E	*LN*	NL	12324	**VE**	TW	*TW*	CP
12310	**TB**	TW	*TW*	CP	12325	**LC**	E	*LN*	NL
12311	**LC**	E	*LN*	NL	12326	**TB**	TW	*TW*	CP
12312	**LC**	E	*LN*	NL	12328	**LC**	E	*LN*	NL
12313	**LC**	E	*LN*	NL	12330	**LC**	E	*LN*	NL

OPEN STANDARD

Mark 4. Air conditioned. Rebuilt with new interior by Bombardier Wakefield 2003–05. Retention toilets. –/76 1T. BT41 bogies. ETS 6X.

Lot No. 31049 Metro-Cammell 1989–92. 40.8 t.

12404	**LC**	E	*LN*	NL	12420	**LC**	E	*LN*	NL
12406	**LC**	E	*LN*	NL	12422	**LC**	E	*LN*	NL
12407	**LC**	E	*LN*	NL	12424	**LC**	E	*LN*	NL
12409	**LC**	E	*LN*	NL	12426	**LC**	E	*LN*	NL

12427	**LC**	E	*LN*	NL	12452	**GC**	TW		LE
12428	**LC**	E	*LN*	NL	12454	**VE**	TW	*TW*	CP
12429	**LC**	E	*LN*	NL	12461	**GC**	TW		LE
12430	**LC**	E	*LN*	NL	12465	**LC**	E	*LN*	NL
12431	**LC**	E	*LN*	NL	12467	**LC**	E	*LN*	NL
12432	**LC**	E	*LN*	NL	12469	**LC**	E	*LN*	NL
12433	**LC**	E	*LN*	NL	12474	**LC**	E	*LN*	NL
12434	**GC**	TW		LE	12477	**GC**	TW		CP
12442	**LC**	E	*LN*	NL	12481	**LC**	E	*LN*	NL
12444	**LC**	E	*LN*	NL	12485	**LC**	E	*LN*	NL
12446	**VE**	TW	*TW*	CP	12515	**LC**	E	*LN*	NL
12447	**VE**	TW	*TW*	CP	12526	**VE**	TW		BK

OPEN STANDARD

Mark 3A. Air conditioned. Rebuilt 2011–13 and fitted with sliding plug doors. Original InterCity 70 seating retained but mainly arranged around tables. Retention toilets. –/72(+6) or * –/69(+4) 1T. BT10 bogies. ETS 6X.

12602–609/614–616/618/620. Lot No. 30877 Derby 1975–77. 36.2 t (* 37.1 t).
12601/613/617–619/621/623/625/627. Lot No. 30878 Derby 1975–76. 36.2 t (* 37.1 t).

12602 (12072)		**CM**	AV	*CR*	AL
12603 (12053)	*	**CM**	AV	*CR*	AL
12604 (12131)		**CM**	AV	*CR*	AL
12605 (11040)	*	**CM**	AV	*CR*	AL
12606 (12048)		**CM**	AV	*CR*	AL
12607 (12038)	*	**CM**	AV	*CR*	AL
12608 (12069)		**CM**	AV	*CR*	AL
12609 (12014)	*	**CM**	AV	*CR*	AL
12610 (12117)		**CM**	AV	*CR*	AL
12613 (11042, 12173)	*	**CM**	AV	*CR*	AL
12614 (12145)		**CM**	AV	*CR*	AL
12615 (12059)	*	**CM**	AV	*CR*	AL
12616 (12127)		**CM**	AV	*CR*	AL
12617 (11052, 12174)	*	**CM**	AV	*CR*	AL
12618 (11008, 12169)		**CM**	AV	*CR*	AL
12619 (11058, 12175)		**CM**	AV	*CR*	AL
12620 (12124)		**CM**	AV	*CR*	AL
12621 (11046)	*	**CM**	AV	*CR*	AL
12623 (11019)	*	**CM**	AV	*CR*	AL
12625 (11030)	*	**CM**	AV	*CR*	AL
12627 (11054)	*	**CM**	AV	*CR*	AL

OPEN STANDARD

CAF Mark 5A. Air conditioned. TransPennine Express coaches. Retention toilets. –/69 1T (* –/59(+6) 1T + bike spaces). CAF bogies. ETS XX.

CAF Beasain 2017–18. 31.8 t (* 31.6 t).

12701		**TP**	BN	*TP*	MA	12721	*	**TP**	BN	*TP*	MA
12702		**TP**	BN	*TP*	MA	12722		**TP**	BN	*TP*	MA
12703	*	**TP**	BN	*TP*	MA	12723		**TP**	BN	*TP*	MA
12704		**TP**	BN	*TP*	MA	12724	*	**TP**	BN	*TP*	MA
12705		**TP**	BN	*TP*	MA	12725		**TP**	BN	*TP*	MA
12706	*	**TP**	BN	*TP*	MA	12726		**TP**	BN	*TP*	MA
12707		**TP**	BN	*TP*	MA	12727	*	**TP**	BN	*TP*	MA
12708		**TP**	BN	*TP*	MA	12728		**TP**	BN	*TP*	MA
12709	*	**TP**	BN	*TP*	MA	12729		**TP**	BN	*TP*	MA
12710		**TP**	BN	*TP*	MA	12730	*	**TP**	BN	*TP*	MA
12711		**TP**	BN	*TP*	MA	12731		**TP**	BN	*TP*	MA
12712	*	**TP**	BN	*TP*	MA	12732		**TP**	BN	*TP*	MA
12713		**TP**	BN	*TP*	MA	12733	*	**TP**	BN	*TP*	MA
12714		**TP**	BN	*TP*	MA	12734		**TP**	BN	*TP*	MA
12715	*	**TP**	BN	*TP*	MA	12735		**TP**	BN	*TP*	MA
12716		**TP**	BN	*TP*	MA	12736	*	**TP**	BN	*TP*	MA
12717		**TP**	BN	*TP*	MA	12737		**TP**	BN	*TP*	MA
12718	*	**TP**	BN	*TP*	MA	12738		**TP**	BN	*TP*	MA
12719		**TP**	BN	*TP*	MA	12739	*	**TP**	BN	*TP*	MA
12720		**TP**	BN	*TP*	MA						

DRIVING OPEN BRAKE STANDARD

CAF Mark 5A. Air conditioned. TransPennine Express coaches. –/64. CAF bogies. ETS XX.

CAF Irun 2017–18. 32.9 t.

12801	**TP**	BN	*TP*	MA	12808	**TP**	BN	*TP*	MA
12802	**TP**	BN	*TP*	MA	12809	**TP**	BN	*TP*	MA
12803	**TP**	BN	*TP*	MA	12810	**TP**	BN	*TP*	MA
12804	**TP**	BN	*TP*	MA	12811	**TP**	BN	*TP*	MA
12805	**TP**	BN	*TP*	MA	12812	**TP**	BN	*TP*	MA
12806	**TP**	BN	*TP*	MA	12813	**TP**	BN	*TP*	MA
12807	**TP**	BN	*TP*	MA	12814	**TP**	BN	*TP*	MA

CORRIDOR FIRST

Mark 1. Seven compartments. 42/– 2T. B4 bogies. ETS 3.

Lot No. 30381 Swindon 1959. 33 t.
Lot No. 30667 Swindon 1962. Commonwealth bogies. 36 t.

13227	x	**CC**	LS	*LS*	CL	13230	xk	**M**	SP	*SP*	BO
13229	xk	**M**	SP	*SP*	BO	13306	x	**M**	WC	*WC*	CS

Name: 13306   JOANNA

OPEN FIRST

Mark 1 converted from Corridor First in 2013–14. 42/– 2T. Commonwealth bogies. ETS 3.

Lot No. 30667 Swindon 1962. 35 t.

13320 x **M** WC *WC* CS ANNA

CORRIDOR FIRST

Mark 2A. Seven compartments. Pressure ventilated. 42/– 2T. B4 bogies. ETS 4.

Lot No. 30774 Derby 1968. 33 t.

13440 v **M** WC *WC* CS

SLEEPER SEATED CARRIAGE WITH BRAKE

CAF Mark 5. Air conditioned. Retention toilets. –/31 1TD 1W. CAF bogies. ETS XX.

CAF Irun 2016–18. 32.5 t.

15001	**CA**	LF	*CA*	PO	15007	**CA**	LF	*CA*	PO
15002	**CA**	LF	*CA*	PO	15008	**CA**	LF	*CA*	PO
15003	**CA**	LF	*CA*	PO	15009	**CA**	LF	*CA*	PO
15004	**CA**	LF	*CA*	PO	15010	**CA**	LF	*CA*	PO
15005	**CA**	LF	*CA*	PO	15011	**CA**	LF	*CA*	PO
15006	**CA**	LF	*CA*	PO					

SLEEPER LOUNGE CAR

CAF Mark 5. Air conditioned. –/30 or –/28 1W. CAF bogies. ETS XX.

CAF Beasain 2016–18. 35.5 t.

15101	**CA**	LF	*CA*	PO	15106	**CA**	LF	*CA*	PO
15102	**CA**	LF	*CA*	PO	15107	**CA**	LF	*CA*	PO
15103	**CA**	LF	*CA*	PO	15108	**CA**	LF	*CA*	PO
15104	**CA**	LF	*CA*	PO	15109	**CA**	LF	*CA*	PO
15105	**CA**	LF	*CA*	PO	15110	**CA**	LF	*CA*	PO

SLEEPING CAR (FULLY ACCESSIBLE)

CAF Mark 5. Air conditioned. Retention toilets. Two fully accessible berths (one with double bed, one with foldable upper bed), two berths with double beds and en-suite toilets and showers, two berths with foldable upper beds. 2TD 2T, plus two showers. CAF bogies. ETS XX.

CAF Castejon/Irun 2016–18. 35.5 t.

15201	**CA**	LF	*CA*	PO	15208	**CA**	LF	*CA*	PO
15202	**CA**	LF	*CA*	PO	15209	**CA**	LF	*CA*	PO
15203	**CA**	LF	*CA*	PO	15210	**CA**	LF	*CA*	PO
15204	**CA**	LF	*CA*	PO	15211	**CA**	LF	*CA*	PO
15205	**CA**	LF	*CA*	PO	15212	**CA**	LF	*CA*	PO
15206	**CA**	LF	*CA*	PO	15213	**CA**	LF	*CA*	PO
15207	**CA**	LF	*CA*	PO	15214	**CA**	LF	*CA*	PO

SLEEPING CAR

CAF Mark 5. Air conditioned. Retention toilets. 6 en-suite toilet/shower and 4 non en-suite compartments with a fixed lower berth and hinged upper berth. 7T. CAF bogies. ETS XX.

CAF Beasain 2016–18. 38.0 t.

15301	**CA**	LF	*CA*	PO	15321	**CA**	LF	*CA*	PO
15302	**CA**	LF	*CA*	PO	15322	**CA**	LF	*CA*	PO
15303	**CA**	LF	*CA*	PO	15323	**CA**	LF	*CA*	PO
15304	**CA**	LF	*CA*	PO	15324	**CA**	LF	*CA*	PO
15305	**CA**	LF	*CA*	PO	15325	**CA**	LF	*CA*	PO
15306	**CA**	LF	*CA*	PO	15326	**CA**	LF	*CA*	PO
15307	**CA**	LF	*CA*	PO	15327	**CA**	LF	*CA*	PO
15308	**CA**	LF	*CA*	PO	15328	**CA**	LF	*CA*	PO
15309	**CA**	LF	*CA*	PO	15329	**CA**	LF	*CA*	PO
15310	**CA**	LF	*CA*	PO	15330	**CA**	LF	*CA*	PO
15311	**CA**	LF	*CA*	PO	15331	**CA**	LF	*CA*	PO
15312	**CA**	LF	*CA*	PO	15332	**CA**	LF	*CA*	PO
15313	**CA**	LF	*CA*	PO	15333	**CA**	LF	*CA*	PO
15314	**CA**	LF	*CA*	PO	15334	**CA**	LF	*CA*	PO
15315	**CA**	LF	*CA*	PO	15335	**CA**	LF	*CA*	PO
15316	**CA**	LF	*CA*	PO	15336	**CA**	LF	*CA*	PO
15317	**CA**	LF	*CA*	PO	15337	**CA**	LF	*CA*	PO
15318	**CA**	LF	*CA*	PO	15338	**CA**	LF	*CA*	PO
15319	**CA**	LF	*CA*	PO	15339	**CA**	LF	*CA*	PO
15320	**CA**	LF	*CA*	PO	15340	**CA**	LF	*CA*	PO

CORRIDOR BRAKE FIRST

Mark 1. Four compartments. 24/– 1T. Commonwealth bogies. ETS 2.

Lot No. 30668 Swindon 1961. 36 t.

17013 (14013)			**CC**	LS	*LS*	CL
17018 (14018)	v		**CH**	VT		TM BOTAURUS

CORRIDOR BRAKE FIRST

Mark 2A. Four compartments. Pressure ventilated. 24/– 1T. B4 bogies. ETS 4.

17090 was numbered 35503 for a time when declassified.

17056. Lot No. 30775 Derby 1967–68. 32 t.
17090/102. Lot No. 30786 Derby 1968. 32 t.

17056 (14056)		**PC**	LS	*LS*	CL
17090 (14090)	v	**CH**	VT		TM
17102 (14102)		**M**	WC	*WC*	CS

COUCHETTE/GENERATOR COACH

Mark 2B. Formerly part of Royal Train. Converted from Corridor Brake First built 1969. Consists of luggage accommodation, guard's compartment, 350 kW diesel generator and staff sleeping accommodation. Pressure ventilated. B5 bogies. ETS 5X (when generator not in use). ETS index ?? (when generator in use).

Lot No. 30888 Wolverton 1977. 46 t.

17105 (14105, 2905)	**BG**	RV	*RV*	BU

CORRIDOR BRAKE FIRST

Mark 2D. Four compartments. Air conditioned. Stones equipment. 24/– 1T. B4 Bogies. ETS 5.

Lot No. 30823 Derby 1971–72. 33.5 t.

17159 (14159)	d	**CC**	LS	*LS*	CL	
17167 (14167)		**VN**	WC	*WC*	CS	MOW COP

OPEN BRAKE UNCLASSIFIED

Mark 3B. Air conditioned. Fitted with hydraulic handbrake. Used as Sleeper day coaches. Refurbished with new Transcal seating 2018. 55/– 1T. BT10 bogies. pg. d. ETS 6X.

Lot No. 30990 Derby 1986. 35.8 t.

17173	**GW**	P	*GW*	PZ		17175	**GW**	P	*GW*	PZ
17174	**GW**	P	*GW*	PZ					

CORRIDOR STANDARD

Mark 1. –/48 2T. Eight Compartments. Commonwealth bogies. ETS 4.

Currently in use as part of the Harry Potter World exhibition at Leavesden, near Watford.

Lot No. 30685 Derby 1961–62. 36 t.

18756 (25756)	x	**M**	WC		Warner Bros, Leavesden

CORRIDOR BRAKE COMPOSITE

Mark 1. There are two variants depending upon whether the Standard Class compartments have armrests. Each vehicle has two First Class and three Standard Class compartments. 12/18 2T (* 12/24 2T). Commonwealth bogies. ETS 2.

21241. Lot No. 30669 Swindon 1961–62. 36 t.
21256. Lot No. 30731 Derby 1963. 37 t.
21266/269. Lot No. 30732 Derby 1964. 37 t.

21241	x	**M**	SP	*SP*	BO	21266	x*	**M**	WC	*WC*	CS
21256	x	**M**	WC	*WC*	CS	21269	*	**CC**	RV		BU

CORRIDOR BRAKE STANDARD

Mark 1. Four compartments. –/24 1T. ETS 2.

35185. Lot No. 30427 Wolverton 1959. B4 bogies. 33 t.
35459/465. Lot No. 30721 Wolverton 1963. Commonwealth bogies. 37 t.

35185	x	**M**	SP	*SP*	BO
35459	x	**M**	WC	*WC*	CS
35465	x	**CC**	LS	*LS*	CL

CORRIDOR BRAKE GENERATOR STANDARD

Mark 1. Four compartments. –/24 1T. Fitted with an ETS generator in the former luggage compartment. ETS 2 (when generator not in use). ETS index ?? (when generator in use).

Lot No. 30721 Wolverton 1963. Commonwealth bogies. 37 t.

35469	x	**CH**	RV	*RV*	BU

BRAKE/POWER KITCHEN

Mark 2C. Pressure ventilated. Converted from Corridor Brake First (declassified to Corridor Brake Standard) built 1970. Converted by West Coast Railway Company 2000–01. Consists of 60 kVA generator, guard's compartment and electric kitchen. B5 bogies. ETS ? (when generator not in use). ETS index ?? (when generator in use).

Non-standard livery: Brown.

Lot No. 30796 Derby 1969–70. 32.5 t.

35511 (14130, 17130)	**0**	LS		CL

KITCHEN CAR

Mark 1. Converted 1989/2006/2017–19 from Kitchen Buffet Unclassified. 80041/020 had buffet and seating area replaced with additional kitchen and food preparation area. 80043 had a full length kitchen fitted. Fluorescent lighting. Commonwealth or (†) B5 bogies. ETS 2X.

Lot No. 30628 Pressed Steel 1960–61. 39 t (* 36.4 t).

80041 (1690)	x	**M**	RV		BU
80042 (1646)		**CH**	RV	*RV*	BU
80043 (1680)	*	**PC**	LS	*LS*	CL
80044 (1659)	†	**CC**	LS	*LS*	CL

DRIVING BRAKE VAN (110 mph)

Mark 3B. Air conditioned. T4 bogies. dg. ETS 5X.

Non-standard livery: 82146 All over silver with DB logos.

Lot No. 31042 Derby 1988. 45.2 t.

82115	**B**	NS		BU		82139	**IC**	LS	*LS*	CL
82127	**IC**	LS	*LS*	CL		82146	**0**	DB	*DB*	TO
82136	**GA**	NS		BU						

Name: 82139 My Lovely Horse

DRIVING BRAKE VAN (140 mph)

Mark 4. Air conditioned. Swiss-built (SIG) bogies. dg. ETS 6X.

Advertising liveries:

82200 Lets we Forget (light blue).
82216 Tŷ Gobaith (Hope House) Children's Hospice (white).
82226 Alzheimer's Society Cymru (blue).
82229 Royal National Lifeboat Institution (black).

Lot No. 31043 Metro-Cammell 1988. 43.5 t.

82200	**AL**	TW	*TW*	CP		82216	**AL**	TW	*TW*	CP
82201	**TB**	TW	*TW*	CP		82218	**VE**	HN		WS
82204	**VE**	TW		LE		82220	**VE**	TW		LE
82205	**LC**	E	*LN*	NL		82222	**LC**	E	*LN*	NL
82208	**LC**	E	*LN*	NL		82223	**LC**	E	*LN*	NL
82210	**VE**	HN		WS		82225	**LC**	E	*LN*	NL
82211	**LC**	E	*LN*	NL		82226	**AL**	TW	*TW*	CP
82212	**LC**	E	*LN*	NL		82227	**TB**	TW	*TW*	CP
82213	**LC**	E	*LN*	NL		82229	**AL**	TW	*TW*	CP
82214	**LC**	E	*LN*	NL		82230	**TB**	TW	*TW*	CP

DRIVING BRAKE VAN (100 mph)

Mark 3B. Air conditioned. T4 bogies. dg. ETS 6X.

82301–305 converted 2008. 82306 converted 2011–12. 82309 converted 2013.

g Fitted with a diesel generator for use while stabled in terminal stations or at depots. 48.5 t.

Lot No. 31042 Derby 1988. 45.2 t.

82301	(82117)	g	**CM**	AV	*CR*	AL
82302	(82151)	g	**CM**	AV	*CR*	AL
82303	(82135)	g	**CM**	AV	*CR*	AL
82304	(82130)	g	**CM**	AV	*CR*	AL
82305	(82134)	g	**CM**	AV	*CR*	AL
82306	(82144)		**AW**	NS		BU
82309	(82104)	g	**CM**	AV	*CR*	AL

GANGWAYED BRAKE VAN (100 mph)

Mark 1. Short frame (57 ft). Load 10 t. Adapted 199? for use as Brake Luggage Van. Guard's compartment retained and former baggage area adapted for secure stowage of passengers' luggage. B4 bogies. 100 mph. ETS 1X.

Lot No. 30162 Pressed Steel 1956–57. 30.5 t.

92904	(80867, 99554)	**VN**	WC	*WC*	CS

HIGH SECURITY GENERAL UTILITY VAN

Mark 1. Short frame (57 ft). Load 14 t. Modified with new floors, three roller shutter doors per side and the end doors removed. Commonwealth bogies. ETS 0X.

Lot No. 30616 Pressed Steel 1959–60. 32 t.

94225	(86849, 93849)	**M**	WC	*WC*	CS

GENERAL UTILITY VAN (100 mph)

Mark 1. Short frame (57 ft). Load 14 t. Screw couplers. Adapted 2013/2010 for use as a water carrier with 3000 gallon capacity. ETS 0.

Non-standard livery: 96100 GWR Brown.

96100. Lot No. 30565 Pressed Steel 1959. 30 t. B5 bogies.
96175. Lot No. 30403 York/Glasgow 1958–60. 32 t. Commonwealth bogies.

96100 (86734, 93734)	x	**0**	VT	*VT*	TM
96175 (86628, 93628)	x	**M**	WC	*WC*	CS

KITCHEN CAR

Mark 1 converted from Corridor First in 2008 with staff accommodation. Commonwealth bogies. ETS 3.

Lot No. 30667 Swindon 1961. 35 t.

99316 (13321)	x	**M**	WC	*WC*	CS

BUFFET STANDARD

Mark 1 converted from Open Standard in 2013 by the removal of two seating bays and fitting of a buffet. –/48 2T. Commonwealth bogies. ETS 4.

Lot No. 30646 Wolverton 1961. 36 t.

99318 (4912)	x	**M**	WC	*WC*	CS

KITCHEN CAR

Mark 1 converted from Corridor Standard in 2011 with staff accommodation. Commonwealth bogies. ETS 3.

Lot No. 30685 Derby 1961–62. 34 t.

99712 (18893)	x	**M**	WC	*WC*	CS

OPEN STANDARD

Mark 1 Corridor Standard rebuilt in 1997 as Open Standard using components from 4936. –/64 2T. Commonwealth bogies. ETS 4.

Lot No. 30685 Derby 1961–62. 36 t.

99722 (25806, 18806)	x	**M**	WC	*WC*	CS

LUL 4 TC USED AS HAULED STOCK

The Class 438 4 TC sets were unpowered units designed to work in push-pull mode with Class 430 (4 Rep) tractor units and Class 33/1, 73 and 74 locomotives. They were converted from locomotive-hauled coaching stock built 1952–57.

The vehicles listed are owned by London Underground and used on both special services on the LU Metropolitan Line and on occasional specials on the National Rail network, top-and-tailed by locomotives.

Mark 1. Trailer Brake Second side corridor with Lavatory (TBSK). Lot No. 30229. Metro-Cammell 1957. 35.5 t.

70823 (34970)   **M**   LU   *WC*   RS

Mark 1. Trailer First side corridor with Lavatory (TFK). Lot No. 30019. Swindon 1954. 33.5 t.

71163 (13097)   **M**   LU   *WC*   RS

Mark 1. Driving Trailer Second Open (DTSO).

76297. Lot No. 30086. Eastleigh 1955. 32.0 t.
76324. Lot No. 30149. Swindon 1956. 32.0 t.

| 76297 | (3938) | **M** | LU | *WC* | RS |
| 76324 | (4009) | **M** | LU | *WC* | RS |

NNR REGISTERED CARRIAGES

These carriages are permitted to operate on the national railway network only between Sheringham and Cromer as an extension of North Norfolk Railway (NNR) "North Norfolkman" services. Only NNR coaches currently registered for use on the national railway network are listed.

KITCHEN BUFFET STANDARD

Mark 1. Built as Unclassified Restaurant. Rebuilt with Buffet Counter and seating reduced. –/23. Commonwealth bogies. Lot No. 30632 Swindon 1960–61. 39 t.

1969   v   **CC**   NN   *NY*   NO

OPEN FIRST

Mark 1. 42/–. Commonwealth bogies. Lot No. 30697 Swindon 1962–63. 36 t.

3116   v   **CC**   NN   *NY*   NO

OPEN STANDARD

Mark 1. –/48 2T. BR Mark 1 bogies. Lot No. 30121 Eastleigh 1953–55. 32 t.

4372   v   **CC**   NN   *NY*   NO

CORRIDOR BRAKE COMPOSITE

Mark 1. Also carried the number DB977580 when in departmental service. 12/18 2T. B4 bogies. Lot No. 30425 Metro-Cammell 1959. 36 t.

21224   v   **CC**   NN   *NY*   NO

GANGWAYED BRAKE VAN

Mark 1. Short frame (57 ft). Now fitted with a kitchen. BR Mark 1 bogies. Lot No. 30224 Cravens 1955–56. 31.5 t.

81033   v   **CC**   NN   *NY*   NO

NYMR REGISTERED CARRIAGES

These carriages are permitted to operate on the national railway network but may only be used to convey fare-paying passengers between Middlesbrough and Whitby on the Esk Valley branch as an extension of North Yorkshire Moors Railway services between Pickering and Grosmont. Only NYMR coaches currently registered for use on the national railway network are listed.

f   Converted to a "fuss free" universal access carriage with new universal access toilet and two wheelchair spaces.

RESTAURANT FIRST

Mark 1. 24/–. Commonwealth bogies. Lot No. 30633 Swindon 1961. 42.5 t.

324	x	**PC**	NY	*NY*		NY		JOS de CRAU

BUFFET STANDARD

Mark 1. –/44 2T. Commonwealth bogies.

1823. Lot No. 30520 Wolverton 1960. 38 t.
1878. Lot No. 30702 Wolverton 1962. 38 t.

1823	v	**M**	NY	*NY*		NY		1878	v	**CC**	NY	*NY*		NY

OPEN STANDARD

Mark 1. –/64 2T (* –/60 2W 2T, † –/60 3W 1T, f –/48 1TD 2W). BR Mark 1 bogies.

3798–3805. Lot No. 30079 York 1953. 33 t.
3860/72. Lot No. 30080 York 1954. 33 t.
3948. Lot No. 30086 Eastleigh 1954–55. 33 t.
4198/4252. Lot No. 30172 York 1956. 33 t.
4286/90. Lot No. 30207 BRCW 1956. 33 t.
4455. Lot No. 30226 BRCW 1957. 33 t.
4597. Lot No. 30243 York 1957. 33 t.

3798	v	**M**	NY	*NY*	NY		4198	v	**M**	NY	*NY*	NY
3801	v	**CC**	NY	*NY*	NY		4252	v*	**CC**	NY	*NY*	NY
3805	fv	**M**	NY	*NY*	NY		4286	v	**CC**	NY	*NY*	NY
3860	v*	**M**	NY	*NY*	NY		4290	v	**M**	NY	*NY*	NY
3872	v†	**M**	NY	*NY*	NY		4455	v	**CC**	NY	*NY*	NY
3948	v	**CC**	NY	*NY*	NY		4597	fv	**CC**	NY	*NY*	NY

OPEN STANDARD

Mark 1. –/48 2T. BR Mark 1 bogies.

4786. Lot No. 30376 York 1957. 33 t.
4817. Lot No. 30473 BRCW 1959. 33 t.

4786	v	**CH**	NY	*NY*		NY		4817	v	**M**	NY	*NY*	NY

OPEN STANDARD

Mark 1. Later vehicles built with Commonwealth bogies. –/64 2T (f –/48 1TD 2W).

Lot No. 30690 Wolverton 1961–62. Aluminium window frames. 37 t.

4921	v	**M**	NY	*NY*	NY		5001	fv	**M**	NY	*NY*	NY
4990	v	**M**	NY	*NY*	NY		5029	v	**M**	NY	*NY*	NY
5000	v	**M**	NY	*NY*	NY							

OPEN BRAKE STANDARD

Mark 1. –/39 1T. BR Mark 1 bogies.

Lot No. 30170 Doncaster 1956. 34 t.

9225	v	**M**	NY	*NY*	NY		9274	v	**M**	NY	*NY*	NY
9235	v	**M**	NY	*NY*	NY							

CORRIDOR COMPOSITE

Mark 1. 24/18 1T. BR Mark 1 bogies.

15745. Lot No. 30179 Metro Cammell 1956. 36 t.
16156/191. Lot No. 30665 Derby 1961. 36 t.

15745	v	**M**	NY	*NY*	NY		16191	v	**M**	NY	*NY*	NY
16156	v	**CC**	NY	*NY*	NY							

CORRIDOR BRAKE COMPOSITE

Mark 1. Two First Class and three Standard Class compartments. 12/18 2T. BR Mark 1 bogies.

Lot No. 30185 Metro Cammell 1956. 36 t.

21100	v	**CC**	NY	*NY*	NY

CORRIDOR BRAKE STANDARD

Mark 1. –/24 1T. BR Mark 1 bogies.

Lot No. 30233 Gloucester 1957. 35 t.

35089 v **CC** NY *NY* NY

PULLMAN BRAKE THIRD

Built 1928 by Metropolitan Carriage & Wagon Company. –/30. Gresley bogies. 37.5 t.

232 v **PC** NY *NY* NY CAR No. 79

PULLMAN KITCHEN FIRST

Built by Metro-Cammell 1960–61 for East Coast Main Line services. 20/– 2T. Commonwealth bogies. 41.2 t.

318 x **PC** NY *NY* NY ROBIN

PULLMAN PARLOUR FIRST

Built by Metro-Cammell 1960–61 for East Coast Main Line services. 29/– 2T. Commonwealth bogies. 38.5 t.

328 x **PC** NY *NY* NY OPAL

2. HIGH SPEED TRAIN TRAILER CARS

HSTs traditionally consist of a number of trailer cars (usually between four and nine) with a power car at each end. All trailers are classified Mark 3 and have BT10 bogies with disc brakes and central door locking. Heating is by a 415 V three-phase supply and vehicles have air conditioning. Maximum speed is 125 mph.

The trailer cars have one standard 23 m bodyshell for both First and Standard Class, thus facilitating easy conversion from one class to the other.

All vehicles underwent a mid-life refurbishment in the 1980s with Standard Class seating layouts revised to incorporate unidirectional seating in addition to facing. A further refurbishment programme was completed in November 2000, with each company having a different scheme as follows:

Great Western Trains (later First Great Western). Green seat covers and extra partitions between seat bays.

Great North Eastern Railway. New lighting panels and brown seat covers.

Virgin CrossCountry. Green seat covers. Standard Class vehicles had four seats in the centre of each carriage replaced with a luggage stack.

Midland Mainline. Grey seat covers, redesigned seat squabs, side carpeting and two seats in the centre of each Standard Class carriage and one in First Class carriages replaced with a luggage stack.

Since then there were many separate, and very different, projects:

Midland Mainline was first to refurbish its vehicles a second time in 2003–04. This involved fitting new fluorescent and halogen ceiling lighting, although the original seats were retained, but with blue upholstery.

East Midlands Trains embarked on another, less radical, refurbishment in 2009–10 which included retention of the original seats but with red upholstery in Standard Class and blue in First. Subsequent operator East Midlands Railway used some former LNER rakes for a time before replacing all of its HSTs in 2021.

First Great Western (now **Great Western Railway**) started a major rebuild of its HST sets in 2006, with the programme completed in 2008. The new interiors featured new lighting and seating. In First Class Primarius seats were used with high-back Grammer seats in Standard Class. A number of sets operated without a full buffet or kitchen car, instead using one of 19 TS vehicles converted to include a "mini buffet" counter for use on shorter distance services. During 2012 15 402xx or 407xx buffet vehicles were converted to Trailer Standards to make the rakes formed as 7-cars up to 8-cars.

Most of the former GWR vehicles have now been scrapped, but GWR has retained a small number of short 4-car sets for local and regional services, although these are expected to be replaced soon. Trailers have been fitted with power doors and renumbered in the 48xxx and 49xxx series'.

Having increased its sets to 9-car sets in 2004, at the end of 2006 **GNER** embarked on a major rebuild of its HSTs. All vehicles have similar interiors to the Mark 4 "Mallard" fleet, with new Primarius seating. The refurbishment of the 13 sets was completed by **National Express East Coast** in late 2009, these trains were later operated by **Virgin Trains East Coast** and then **London North Eastern Railway**. VTEC refurbished its sets in 2015–16, with the same seats retained but with new upholstery, and leather in First Class, but all sets were taken out of traffic with LNER by the end of 2019.

Open access operator **Grand Central** started operation in December 2007 with a new service from Sunderland to London King's Cross. This operator had three sets mostly using stock converted from loco-hauled Mark 3s. The seats in Standard Class have First Class spacing and in most vehicles are all facing. These sets were withdrawn in December 2017 and transferred to East Midlands Trains (then EMR). They were refurbished in 2018–19, with ex-GWR buffet cars used instead of the original Grand Central buffet cars.

CrossCountry reintroduced HSTs to the Cross-Country network from 2008. Five sets were refurbished at Wabtec, Doncaster principally for use on the Plymouth–Edinburgh route. Three of these sets use stock mostly converted from loco-hauled Mark 3s and two are sets ex-Midland Mainline. The interiors are similar to refurbished East Coast sets, although the seating layout is different and one toilet per carriage has been removed in favour of a luggage stack. These sets were later fitted with sliding power doors but were withdrawn in 2023.

ScotRail started operating HSTs from October 2018. The operator has a fleet of 25 sets, of which five are 5-cars and the rest are 4-cars, but it is planned to make more up to five carriages. They have been fitted with sliding power doors for use between Glasgow/Edinburgh and Aberdeen/Inverness, and on the Aberdeen–Inverness route.

Crewe-based **Locomotive Services** has acquired a number of former GWR and EMR HST vehicles and power cars. It uses its premium "Midland Pullman" set in a striking blue livery on luxury trips and also formed a second rake in 2021 for Rail Charter Services in green/silver livery, but this has now been disbanded. The **125 Group** also plans to return its rake of trailers and its power cars to the main line. The future for many of the other remaining vehicles appears to be export – with one HST set shipped to Mexico in summer 2023 and others set to follow.

Operator Codes

Operator codes are shown in the heading before each set of vehicles. The first letter is always "T" for HST carriages, denoting a Trailer vehicle. The second letter denotes the passenger accommodation in that vehicle, for example "F" for First. "GS" denotes Guards accommodation and Standard Class seating. This is followed by catering provision, with "B" for buffet, and "K" for a kitchen and buffet:

TC	Trailer Composite		TGFB	Trailer Guard's Buffet First
TCK	Trailer Composite Kitchen		TSB	Trailer Buffet Standard
TF	Trailer First		TS	Trailer Standard
TFB	Trailer Buffet First		TGF	Trailer Guard's First
TFKB	Trailer Kitchen Buffet First		TGS	Trailer Guard's Standard

Power doors: All HSTs now operated by Great Western Railway and ScotRail (and also those withdrawn by CrossCountry in 2023) have been fitted with power sliding doors and retention toilets. Vehicles so fitted are shown with a "p" in the Notes column.

TRAILER BUFFET STANDARD   TSB

19 vehicles (40101–119) were converted at Laira 2009–10 from HST TSs for First Great Western. All other vehicles now scrapped. Grammer seating.

40106. Lot No. 30897 Derby 1977–79. –/70 1T. 35.5 t.

40106 (42162)   **FD**   LS   KR

TRAILER BUFFET FIRST   TFB

Converted from TSB by fitting First Class seats. Renumbered from 404xx series by subtracting 200. Refurbished by First Great Western and fitted with Primarius leather seating. 23/–.

Lot No. 30883 Derby 1976–77. 36.12 t.

40221   **EA**   LS   CL |

TRAILER GUARD'S MINIATURE BUFFET FIRST TGFB

Refurbished 2018–21 for ScotRail. Former Great Western Railway vehicles. Primarius seating. Fitted with a new corner buffet counter and kitchen. 32/– 1T.

40601–626. For Lot No. details see TF. 39.1 t.

40601	(41032) p	**SI**	A	*SR*	IS	40614	(41010) p	**SI**	A	*SR*	IS
40602	(41038) p	**SI**	A		ZB	40615	(41022) p	**SI**	A	*SR*	IS
40603	(41006) p	**SI**	A	*SR*	IS	40616	(41142) p	**SI**	A	*SR*	IS
40604	(41024) p	**SI**	A	*SR*	IS	40617	(41144) p	**SI**	A	*SR*	IS
40605	(41094) p	**SI**	A	*SR*	IS	40618	(41016) p	**SI**	A	*SR*	IS
40606	(41104) p	**SI**	A	*SR*	IS	40619	(41124) p	**SI**	A	*SR*	IS
40607	(41136) p	**SI**	A	*SR*	IS	40620	(41158) p	**SI**	A	*SR*	IS
40608	(41122) p	**SI**	A		ZB	40621	(41146) p	**SI**	A	*SR*	IS
40609	(41020) p	**SI**	A	*SR*	IS	40623	(41180) p	**SI**	A		ZB
40610	(41103) p	**SI**	A	*SR*	IS	40624	(41116) p	**SI**	A	*SR*	IS
40611	(41130) p	**SI**	A	*SR*	IS	40625	(41137) p	**SI**	A	*SR*	IS
40612	(41134) p	**SI**	A	*SR*	IS	40626	(41012) p	**SI**	A	*SR*	IS
40613	(41135) p	**SI**	A	*SR*	IS						

TRAILER KITCHEN BUFFET FIRST   TFKB

These vehicles have larger kitchens than the 402xx and 404xx series vehicles, and are used in trains where a full meal service is required. They were renumbered from the 403xx series (in which the seats were unclassified) by adding 400 to the previous number. 17/–.

* Refurbished former GWR vehicles. Primarius leather seating.
m Refurbished former LNER vehicles with Primarius leather seating.

40715. Lot No. 30921 Derby 1978–79. 38.16 t.
40728–734. Lot No. 30940 Derby 1979–80. 38.16 t.
40741/750. Lot No. 30948 Derby 1980–81. 38.16 t.
40755. Lot No. 30966 Derby 1982. 38.16 t.

40715	*	**GW**	A	EP	40741	**ST**	125	RD
40728		**ST**	NS	BU	40750	m	**VE**	A	EP
40730		**ST**	125	LB	40755	*	**GW**	A	ZG
40734	*	**FD**	A	EP				

TRAILER KITCHEN BUFFET FIRST   TFKB

These vehicles have been converted from TSBs in the 404xx series to be similar to the 407xx series vehicles. 17/–. Primarius leather seating.

40802 and 40804 were numbered 40212 and 40232 for a time when fitted with 23 First Class seats.

40801/802/808. Lot No. 30883 Derby 1976–77. 38.16 t.
40804. Lot No. 30899 Derby 1978–79. 38.16 t.

40801	(40027, 40427)	**MP**	LS	*LS*	CL
40802	(40012, 40412)	**MP**	LS	*LS*	CL
40804	(40032, 40432)	**RC**	LS	*LS*	CL
40808	(40015, 40415)	**FD**	LS		ZG

TRAILER BUFFET FIRST   TFB

Converted from TSB by First Great Western. Refurbished with Primarius leather seating. 23/–.

Lot No. 30883 Derby 1976–77. 36.12 t.

40902	(40023, 40423)	**FD**	FG		ZG

TRAILER FIRST   TF

As built and m 48/– 2T (m† 48/– 1T – one toilet removed for trolley space).
* Refurbished former GWR vehicles. Primarius leather seating.
m Refurbished former LNER vehicles with Primarius leather seating.
px Refurbished former CrossCountry vehicles with power doors, Primarius seating and one toilet removed. 39/– 1TD 1W.
s Fitted with centre luggage stack, disabled toilet and wheelchair space. 46/– 1TD 1T 1W.
w Wheelchair space. 47/– 2T 1W.

41026/035. Lot No. 30881 Derby 1976–77. 33.66 t.
41057–117. Lot No. 30896 Derby 1977–78. 33.66 t.
41149–166. Lot No. 30947 Derby 1980. 33.66 t.
41167/169. Lot No. 30963 Derby 1982. 33.66 t.
41176. Lot No. 30897 Derby 1977. 33.66 t.
41182/183. Lot No. 30939 Derby 1979–80. 33.66 t.
41187. Lot No. 30969 Derby 1982. 33.66 t.
41193/194. Lot No. 30878 Derby 1975–76. 34.3 t. Converted from Mark 3A Open First.
41208. Lot No. 30877 Derby 1975–77. Converted from Mark 3A Open Standard.

41026	px	**XC**	A	YA	41059	*w	**MP**	LS	*LS*	CL
41035	px	**XC**	A	YA	41063		**ST**	LS	*LS*	CL
41057		**ST**	125	RD	41067	s	**ST**	125	RD

41087	m†	**VE**	A			EP		41160	*w	**RC**	LS	*LS*		CL
41106	*w	**FD**	A			ZG		41162	*w	**MP**	LS	*LS*		CL
41108	*w	**MP**	LS	*LS*		CL		41166	*w	**RC**	LS	*LS*		CL
41117		**ST**	LS	*LS*		CL		41167	*w	**FD**	LS			ZG
41149	*w	**MP**	LS	*LS*		CL		41169	*w	**MP**	LS	*LS*		CL

41176	(42142, 42352)	*w	**MP**	LS *LS*	CL
41182	(42278)	*w	**MP**	LS *LS*	CL
41183	(42274)	*w	**MP**	LS *LS*	CL
41187	(42311)	*w	**RC**	LS *LS*	CL

The following carriages were converted from loco-hauled Mark 3 vehicles.

41193	(11060)	px	**XC**	P	BH
41194	(11016)	px	**XC**	P	LM
41208	(12112, 42406)	w	**EA**	LS	ZG

TRAILER STANDARD   TS

Standard seating and m –/76 2T.
* Refurbished former Great Western Railway vehicles. Grammer seating. –/80 2T (unless h – high density).
h "High density" former Great Western Railway vehicles. –/84 2T.
k "High density" former Great Western Railway refurbished vehicle with disabled persons toilet and 5, 6 or 7 tip-up seats. –/72 1T 1TD 2W.
m Refurbished former LNER vehicles with Primarius seating.
pr Refurbished ScotRail vehicles with power doors and Grammer seating. –/68(+6).
ps Refurbished ScotRail vehicles with power doors and Grammer seating. –/74 1T.
p* Refurbished ScotRail vehicles with power doors, Grammer seating and universal access toilet. –/58 1TD 2W.
px Refurbished former CrossCountry vehicles with power doors and Primarius seating. –/80 1T.
pt Refurbished former CrossCountry vehicles with power doors, Primarius seating and universal access toilet. –/64 1TD 2W.
u Centre luggage stack (EMR) –/74 2T.
w Centre luggage stack and wheelchair space (EMR) –72 2T 1W.
† Disabled persons toilet (LNER) –/62 1T 1TD 1W.

42004–078. Lot No. 30882 Derby 1976–77. 33.6 t.
42096–250. Lot No. 30897 Derby 1977–79. 33.6 t.
42252–301. Lot No. 30939 Derby 1979–80. 33.6 t.
42319. Lot No. 30969 Derby 1982. 33.6 t.
42325–337. Lot No. 30983 Derby 1984–85. 33.6 t.
42342/360. Lot No. 30949 Derby 1982. 33.47 t. Converted from TGS.
42343/345. Lot No. 30970 Derby 1982. 33.47 t. Converted from TGS.
42247/350/351/379/380/551–562. Lot No. 30881 Derby 1976–77. 33.66 t. Converted from TF.
42363/567–569. Lot No. 30896 Derby 1977–78. 33.66 t. Converted from TF.

42366–378/404/408. Lot No. 30877 Derby 1975–77. 34.3 t. Converted from Mark 3A Open Standard.
42506. Lot No. 30940 Derby 1979–80. 34.8 t. Converted from TFKB.
42571–579. Lot No. 30938 Derby 1979–80. 33.66 t. Converted from TF.
42581/583. Lot No. 30947 Derby 1980. 33.66 t. Converted from TF.
42584/585. Lot No. 30878 Derby 1975–76. Converted from Mark 3A Open First.

No.					
42004	p*	SI	A	SR	IS
42009	ps	SI	A	SR	IS
42010	ps	SI	A	SR	IS
42012	p*	SI	A	SR	IS
42013	ps	SI	A	SR	IS
42014	ps	SI	A	SR	IS
42019	ps	SI	A		ZB
42021	p*	SI	A	SR	IS
42023	ps	SI	A	SR	IS
42024	*k	FD	A		EP
42029	ps	SI	A	SR	IS
42030	p*	SI	A	SR	IS
42032	ps	SI	A	SR	IS
42033	ps	SI	A	SR	IS
42034	pr	SI	A	SR	IS
42035	ps	SI	A	SR	IS
42036	px	XC	A		EP
42037	px	XC	A		YA
42038	px	XC	A		EP
42045	ps	SI	A		ZB
42046	ps	SI	A	SR	IS
42047	ps	SI	A	SR	IS
42051	px	XC	A		YA
42052	px	XC	A		EP
42053	px	XC	A		EP
42054	ps	SI	A	SR	IS
42055	p*	SI	A		ZB
42056	ps	SI	A	SR	IS
42072	pr	SI	A	SR	IS
42075	ps	SI	A	SR	IS
42077	ps	SI	A	SR	IS
42078	ps	SI	A	SR	IS
42096	ps	SI	A	SR	IS
42097	px	XC	A		EP
42100	u	ST	LS	LS	CL
42107	pr	SI	A	SR	IS
42110	m	VE	NS		BU
42111	u	ST	125		RD
42119	u	ST	125		RD
42120	u	ST	125		RD
42129	ps	SI	A	SR	IS
42143	ps	SI	A	SR	IS
42144	ps	SI	A	SR	IS
42183	p*	SI	A	SR	IS
42184	ps	SI	A	SR	IS
42185	ps	SI	A	SR	IS
42200	p*	SI	A	SR	IS
42206	p*	SI	A	SR	IS
42207	p*	SI	A	SR	IS
42208	ps	SI	A	SR	IS
42209	ps	SI	A	SR	IS
42213	ps	SI	A	SR	IS
42220	w	ST	LS	LS	CL
42234	px	XC	P		BH
42245	pr	SI	A	SR	IS
42250	ps	SI	A	SR	IS
42252	ps	SI	A	SR	IS
42253	p*	SI	A	SR	IS
42255	p*	SI	A	SR	IS
42256	ps	SI	A	SR	IS
42257	ps	SI	A	SR	IS
42259	p*	SI	A	SR	IS
42265	p*	SI	A	SR	IS
42267	p*	SI	A	SR	IS
42268	p*	SI	A	SR	IS
42269	p*	SI	A	SR	IS
42275	p*	SI	A		ZB
42276	ps	SI	A		ZB
42277	ps	SI	A	SR	IS
42279	p*	SI	A	SR	IS
42280	pr	SI	A	SR	IS
42281	p*	SI	A	SR	IS
42288	ps	SI	A	SR	IS
42290	px	XC	P		BH
42291	p*	SI	A	SR	IS
42292	p*	SI	A		ZB
42293	ps	SI	A	SR	IS
42295	p*	SI	A	SR	IS
42296	ps	SI	A	SR	IS
42297	p*	SI	A	SR	IS
42299	ps	SI	A	SR	IS
42300	pr	SI	A	SR	IS
42301	ps	SI	A	SR	IS
42319	*h	GW	LS		KR
42325	pr	SI	A	SR	IS
42333	ps	SI	A	SR	IS
42337	w	ST	125		RD

42342	(44082)	px	**XC**	A		YA
42343	(44095)	ps	**SI**	A	*SR*	IS
42345	(44096)	p*	**SI**	A	*SR*	IS
42347	(41054)	*k	**FD**	A		EP
42350	(41047)	ps	**SI**	A	*SR*	IS
42351	(41048)	ps	**SI**	A	*SR*	IS
42360	(44084, 45084)	p*	**SI**	A	*SR*	IS

42366–378 were converted from loco-hauled Mark 3 vehicles for CrossCountry.

42366	(12007)	pt	**XC**	P		BH
42368	(12028)	px	**XC**	P		BH
42369	(12050)	px	**XC**	P		BH
42370	(12086)	px	**XC**	P		LM
42371	(12052)	pt	**XC**	P		BH
42372	(12055)	px	**XC**	P		BH
42373	(12071)	px	**XC**	P		BH
42375	(12113)	px	**XC**	P		Reid's, Stoke
42376	(12085)	pt	**XC**	P		BH
42377	(12102)	px	**XC**	P		LM
42378	(12123)	px	**XC**	P		BH
42379	(41036)	pt	**XC**	A		YA
42380	(41025)	pt	**XC**	A		EP

These carriages were converted from loco-hauled Mark 3 vehicles for Grand Central. They have a lower density seating layout (most seats arranged around tables). –/62 2T.

42404	(12152)		**EA**	A		EP
42408	(12121)		**EA**	A		EP

Converted from TFKB or TSB buffet cars to TS vehicles in 2011–12 at Wabtec Kilmarnock for FGW. Refurbished with Grammer seating. –/84 1T. 34.8 t.

42506	(40324, 40724)		**FD**	A		EP

These carriages were converted from TF to TS vehicles in 2014 at Wabtec Kilmarnock for FGW. Refurbished with Grammer seating. –/80 1T (pr –/68(+6). 35.5 t.

42551	(41003)	pr	**SI**	A	*SR*	IS
42553	(41009)	pr	**SI**	A	*SR*	IS
42555	(41015)	pr	**SI**	A	*SR*	IS
42557	(41019)	pr	**SI**	A	*SR*	IS
42558	(41021)	pr	**SI**	A	*SR*	IS
42559	(41023)	pr	**SI**	A	*SR*	IS
42561	(41031)	pr	**SI**	A	*SR*	IS
42562	(41037)	pr	**SI**	A		ZB
42567	(41093)	pr	**SI**	A	*SR*	IS
42568	(41101)	pr	**SI**	A	*SR*	IS
42569	(41105)		**FD**	A		EP
42571	(41121)	pr	**SI**	A		ZB
42574	(41129)	pr	**SI**	A	*SR*	IS
42575	(41131)	pr	**SI**	A	*SR*	IS

42576	(41133)	pr	**SI**	A		ZB
42577	(41141)	pr	**SI**	A	*SR*	IS
42578	(41143)	pr	**SI**	A	*SR*	IS
42579	(41145)	pr	**SI**	A	*SR*	IS
42581	(41157)	pr	**SI**	A	*SR*	IS
42583	(41153, 42385)		**GW**	LS		KR

These carriages were converted from loco-hauled carriages for Grand Central, before being converted to TS for East Midlands Railway. –/62 2T.

42584	(11045, 41201)	**EA**	A		EP
42585	(11017, 41202)	**EA**	A		EP

TRAILER GUARD'S STANDARD/FIRST TGS/TGF

As built and m –/65 1T.
* Refurbished Great Western Railway vehicles. Grammer seating and toilet removed for trolley store. –/67 (unless h).
† Converted to Trailer Guard's First (TGF) with Primarius seating. 36/–.
p Refurbished former CrossCountry vehicles with power doors and Primarius seating. –/67.
h "High density" Great Western Railway vehicles. –/71.
s Fitted with centre luggage stack (EMR) –/63 1T.

44000. Lot No. 30953 Derby 1980. 33.47 t.
44012–081. Lot No. 30949 Derby 1980–82. 33.47 t.

44000	*h	**GW**	125		RD		44052	p	**XC**	P		BH
44012	p	**XC**	A		EP		44072	p	**XC**	P		BH
44017	p	**XC**	A		EP		44078	†	**MP**	LS	*LS*	CL
44021	p	**XC**	P		LM		44081	†	**MP**	LS	*LS*	CL
44047	s	**ST**	LS	*LS*	CL							

TRAILER COMPOSITE KITCHEN TCK

Converted from Mark 3A Open Standard. Refurbished former CrossCountry vehicles with Primarius seating. Small kitchen for the preparation of hot food and stowage space for two trolleys between First and Standard Class. One toilet removed. 30/8 1T.

45001–005. Lot No. 30877 Derby 1975–77. 34.3 t.

45001	(12004)	p	**XC**	P	BH
45002	(12106)	p	**XC**	P	BH
45003	(12076)	p	**XC**	P	BH
45004	(12077)	p	**XC**	P	BH
45005	(12080)	p	**XC**	P	BH

TRAILER COMPOSITE   TC

Converted from TF for First Great Western 2014–15. Refurbished with Grammer seating. 24/39 1T.

46006. Lot No. 30896 Derby 1977–78. 35.6 t. Converted from TF.
46012. Lot No. 30938 Derby 1979–80. 35.6 t. Converted from TF.
46014. Lot No. 30963 Derby 1982. 35.6 t. Converted from TF.

46006	(41081)	**FD**	LS		ZG
46012	(41147)	**FD**	LS		KR
46014	(41168)	**CC**	LS *LS*	CL	MOIDART

TRAILER STANDARD   TS

Refurbished for Great Western Railway 2017–21 and fitted with power doors and retention toilets. Used in 4-car sets on local and regional services across the South-West. –/84 1T († –/62 + 5 tip-ups 1TD 2W).

48101–137/140–150. For Lot No. details see TS. 36.3 t.

48101	(42093, 48111)	p	**GW**	FG	YA
48102	(42218)	p†	**GW**	FG *GW*	LA
48103	(42168, 48101)	p	**GW**	FG	YA
48104	(41107, 42365)	p	**GW**	FG *GW*	LA
48105	(42266)	p†	**GW**	FG *GW*	LA
48106	(42258)	p	**GW**	FG *GW*	LA
48107	(42101)	p	**GW**	FG *GW*	LA
48108	(42174)	p†	**GW**	FG *GW*	LA
48109	(42085)	p	**GW**	FG *GW*	LA
48110	(42315)	p	**GW**	FG	LA
48111	(42224)	p†	**GW**	FG	LA
48112	(42222)	p	**GW**	FG	LA
48113	(42177, 48102)	p	**GW**	FG	YA
48114	(42317)	p†	**GW**	FG *GW*	LA
48115	(42285)	p	**GW**	A	YA
48117	(42271)	p†	**GW**	A *GW*	LA
48118	(42073)	p	**GW**	A *GW*	LA
48119	(42204)	p	**GW**	A *GW*	LA
48120	(42201)	p†	**GW**	A *GW*	LA
48121	(42027)	p	**GW**	A *GW*	LA
48122	(42214)	p	**GW**	A *GW*	LA
48123	(42211)	p†	**GW**	A *GW*	LA
48124	(42212)	p	**GW**	A *GW*	LA
48125	(42203)	p	**GW**	A	YA
48126	(42138)	p†	**GW**	A *GW*	LA
48127	(42349)	p	**GW**	A	EP
48128	(42044)	p	**GW**	A	EP
48129	(42008)	p†	**GW**	A	EP
48130	(42102, 48131)	p	**GW**	FG *GW*	LA
48131	(42042)	p	**GW**	A	YA

48132	(42202)	p†	**GW**	A	YA
48133	(42003)	p	**GW**	A	YA
48136	(41114, 42570)	p	**GW**	FG *GW*	LA
48137	(41163, 42582)	p	**GW**	FG *GW*	LA
48140	(42005)	p	**GW**	GW	YA
48141	(42015)	p†	**GW**	GW	YA
48142	(42016)	p	**GW**	GW	YA
48143	(42050)	p	**GW**	GW	EP
48144	(42066)	p†	**GW**	GW	EP
48145	(42048)	p	**GW**	GW	EP
48146	(42074)	p	**GW**	GW	EP
48147	(42081)	p†	**GW**	GW	EP
48148	(42071)	p	**GW**	GW	EP
48149	(42087)	p	**GW**	GW *GW*	LA
48150	(42580)	p	**GW**	GW *GW*	LA

TRAILER GUARD'S STANDARD   TGS

Refurbished for Great Western Railway 2017–21 and fitted with power doors. –/71.

49101–117. For Lot No. details see TGS. 35.7 t.

49101	(44055)	p	**GW**	FG	YA
49102	(44083)	p	**GW**	FG *GW*	LA
49103	(44097)	p	**GW**	FG *GW*	LA
49104	(44101)	p	**GW**	FG	LA
49105	(44090)	p	**GW**	FG *GW*	LA
49106	(44033)	p	**GW**	A *GW*	LA
49107	(44064)	p	**GW**	A	YA
49108	(44067)	p	**GW**	A *GW*	LA
49109	(44003)	p	**GW**	A *GW*	LA
49110	(44014)	p	**GW**	A	EP
49111	(44036)	p	**GW**	A	YA
49112	(44079)	p	**GW**	FG	LA
49114	(44005)	p	**GW**	GW	YA
49115	(44016)	p	**GW**	GW	EP
49116	(44002)	p	**GW**	GW	EP
49117	(44042)	p	**GW**	GW *GW*	LA

HST SET FORMATIONS

GREAT WESTERN RAILWAY

GWR has been reducing its number of short 4-car HST sets since 2022 – from 16 sets down to seven at the time of writing. These trains are used on regional and local services in the South-West.

Number of sets: 7.   **Maximum number of daily diagrams:** 4.
Formations: 4-cars.   **Allocation:** Laira (Plymouth).
Other maintenance and servicing depots: Long Rock (Penzance), St Philip's Marsh (Bristol).
Operation: Bristol–Exeter–Plymouth–Penzance and Cardiff–Bristol–Taunton.

Set	D	C	B	A
GW02	48106	48105	48104	49102
GW03	48109	48108	48107	49103
GW05	48130	48114	48102	49105
GW06	48118	48117	48136	49106
GW07	48121	48120	48119	49108
GW08	48124	48123	48122	49117
GW09	48137	48126	48150	49109

Spare:

LA:	48149

SCOTRAIL

ScotRail has introduced refurbished HSTs onto its Edinburgh/Glasgow–Aberdeen/Inverness services – branded INTER-7-CITY as they serve Scotland's seven cities. It is ultimately planned that there will be 17 5-car and eight 4-car sets (HA22 was written off in the 2020 Carmont accident). The first 5-car sets were introduced in 2021 and further 4-cars sets will be lengthened to 5-cars as passenger demand dictates. Sets HA02, HA08 and HA23 are currently stood down at Wabtec, Doncaster Works.

Number of sets: 25.
Maximum number of daily diagrams: 16.
Formations: 4-cars or 5-cars.
Allocation: Power cars: Haymarket (Edinburgh), Trailers: Inverness.
Operation: Edinburgh/Glasgow–Aberdeen, Edinburgh/Glasgow–Inverness, Aberdeen–Inverness.

Set	A	B	C	D	E	
HA01	40601	42004	42561	42046		
HA02	40602	42292	42562	42045		*(stored at Wabtec, Doncaster)*
HA03	40603	42021	42557	42143		
HA04	40604	42183	42559	42343		
HA05	40605	42345	42034	42184	42029	
HA06	40606	42206	42581	42208	42033	
HA07	40607	42207	42574	42288	42056	
HA08	40608	42055	42571	42019		*(stored at Wabtec, Doncaster)*
HA09	40609	42253	42107	42257		
HA10	40610	42360	42551	42252	42351	
HA11	40611	42267	42325	42301	42023	
HA12	40612	42275	42576	42276		
HA13	40613	42279	42296	42296		
HA14	40614	42012	42245	42013		
HA15	40615	42030	42579	42010		
HA16	40616	42291	42577	42075		
HA17	40617	42295	42558	42250		
HA18	40618	42297	42555	42014		
HA19	40619	42255	42568	42256		
HA20	40620	42200	42575	42129		
HA21	40621	42299	42300	42277		
HA23	40623	42268	42567	42269		*(stored at Wabtec, Doncaster)*
HA24	40624	42265	42553	42293		
HA25	40625	42259	42578	42333		
HA26	40626	42281	42072	42350		

Extra coaches that have been refurbished to make further sets up to 5-car rakes:

42009 42032 42035 42047 42054 42077 42078 42096 42144
42185 42209 42213

3. SALOONS

Several specialist passenger carrying carriages, normally referred to as saloons are permitted to run on the national railway system. Many of these are to pre-nationalisation designs.

WCJS FIRST CLASS SALOON

Built 1892 by LNWR, Wolverton. Originally dining saloon mounted on six-wheel bogies. Rebuilt with new underframe with four-wheel bogies in 1927. Rebuilt 1960 as observation saloon with DMU end. Gangwayed at other end. The interior has a saloon, kitchen, guards vestibule and observation lounge. 19/– 1T. Gresley bogies. 28.5 t. 75 mph. ETS x.

41   (484, 45018) x   **M**   WC   *WC*   CS

LNWR DINING SALOON

Built 1890 by LNWR, Wolverton. Mounted on the underframe of LMS General Utility Van 37908 in the 1980s. Contains kitchen and dining area seating 12 at tables for two. 12/–. Gresley bogies. 75 mph. 25.4 t. ETS x.

159   (5159)   x   **M**   WC   *WC*   CS

GNR FIRST CLASS SALOON

Built 1912 by GNR, Doncaster. Contains entrance vestibule, lavatory, two separate saloons, library and luggage space. 19/– 1T. Gresley bogies. 75 mph. 29.4 t. ETS x.

Non-standard livery: Teak.

807   (4807)   x   **0**   WC   *WC*   CS

LNER GENERAL MANAGERS SALOON

Built 1945 by LNER, York. Gangwayed at one end with a veranda at the other. The interior has a dining saloon seating 12, kitchen, toilet, office and nine seat lounge. 21/– 1T. B4 bogies. 75 mph. 35.7 t. ETS 3.

1999   (902260)   **M**   WC   CS   DINING CAR No. 2

GENERAL MANAGER'S SALOON

Renumbered 1989 from London Midland Region departmental series. Formerly the LMR General Manager's saloon. Rebuilt from LMS period 1 Corridor Brake First M5033M to dia 1654 and mounted on the underframe of BR suburban Brake Standard M43232. Screw couplings have been removed. B4 bogies. 100 mph. ETS 2X.

LMS Lot No. 326 Derby 1927. 27.5 t.

6320   (5033, DM 395707)   x   **M**   PR   *PR*   SK

SUPPORT CAR

Converted 199? from Courier vehicle converted from Mark 1 Corridor Brake Standard 1986–87. Toilet retained and former compartment area replaced with train manager's office, crew locker room, linen store and dry goods store. The former luggage area has been adapted for use as an engineers' compartment and workshop. B5 bogies. 100 mph. ETS 2.

Lot No. 30721 Wolverton 1963. 35.5 t.

99545 (35466, 80207)   **PC**   BE   *BP*   SL   BAGGAGE CAR No. 11

SERVICE CAR

Converted from BR Mark 1 Corridor Brake Standard. Commonwealth bogies. 100 mph. ETS 2.

Lot No. 30721 Wolverton 1963.

99886 (35407)   x   **M** WC   *WC*   CS   86   SERVICE CAR No. 1

ROYAL SCOTSMAN SALOONS

Built 1960 by Metro-Cammell as Pullman Kitchen Second for East Coast Main Line Services. Rebuilt 2016 as a Spa Car with two large bedrooms with bathroom/spa areas. Commonwealth bogies. xx t. ETS ?.

99337 (CAR No. 337)   **M** BE   *RS*   HN   STATE SPA CAR

Built 1960 by Metro-Cammell as Pullman Kitchen First for East Coast Main Line services. Rebuilt 2013 as dining car. Commonwealth bogies. 38.5 t. ETS ?.

99960 (321 SWIFT)   **M** BE   *RS*   HN   DINING CAR No. 2

Built 1960 by Metro-Cammell as Pullman Parlour First (§ Pullman Kitchen First) for East Coast Main Line services. Rebuilt 1990 as sleeping cars with four twin sleeping rooms (*§ three twin sleeping rooms and two single sleeping rooms at each end). Commonwealth bogies. 38.5 t. ETS ?.

99961	(324 AMBER) *	**M**	BE	*RS*	HN	STATE CAR No. 1
99962	(329 PEARL)	**M**	BE	*RS*	HN	STATE CAR No. 2
99963	(331 TOPAZ)	**M**	BE	*RS*	HN	STATE CAR No. 3
99964	(313 FINCH) §	**M**	BE	*RS*	HN	STATE CAR No. 4

Built 1960 by Metro-Cammell as Pullman Kitchen First for East Coast Main Line services. Rebuilt 1990 as observation car with open verandah seating 32. B4 bogies. 36.95 t. ETS ?.

| 99965 | (319 SNIPE) | **M** | BE | *RS* | HN | OBSERVATION CAR |

Built 1960 by Metro-Cammell as Pullman Kitchen First for East Coast Main Line services. Rebuilt 1993 as dining car. Commonwealth bogies. 38.5 t. ETS ?.

| 99967 | (317 RAVEN) | **M** | BE | *RS* | HN | DINING CAR No. 1 |

Mark 3A. Converted 1997 from a Sleeping Car at Carnforth Railway Restoration & Engineering Services. BT10 bogies. Attendant's and adjacent two sleeping compartments converted to generator room containing a 160 kW Volvo unit. In 99968 four sleeping compartments remain for staff use with another converted for use as a staff shower and toilet. The remaining five sleeping compartments have been replaced by two passenger cabins. In 99969 seven sleeping compartments remain for staff use. A further sleeping compartment, along with one toilet, have been converted to store rooms. The other two sleeping compartments have been combined to form a crew mess. 41.5 t. 99968 ETS index ?. 99969 ETS 7X (when generator not in use). ETS index ?? (when generator in use).

Lot No. 30960 Derby 1981–83.

| 99968 | (10541) | **M** | BE | *RS* | HN | STATE CAR No. 5 |
| 99969 | (10556) | **M** | BE | *RS* | HN | SERVICE CAR |

"CLUB CAR"

Converted from BR Mark 1 Open Standard at Carnforth Railway Restoration & Engineering Services in 1994. Contains kitchen, pantry and two dining saloons. 20/– 1T. Commonwealth bogies. 100 mph. ETS 4.

Lot No. 30724 York 1963. 37 t.

| 99993 | (5067) | x | **CC** | LS | *LS* | CL | CLUB CAR |

BR INSPECTION SALOON

Mark 1. Short frames. Non-gangwayed. Observation windows at each end. The interior layout consists of two saloons interspersed by a central lavatory/kitchen/guards/luggage section. 90 mph. ETS x.

BR Wagon Lot No. 3095 Swindon 1957. B4 bogies. 30.5 t.

| 999506 | | **M** | WC | *WC* | CS | |

4. PULLMAN CAR COMPANY SERIES

Pullman cars have never generally been numbered as such, although many have carried numbers, instead they have carried titles. However, a scheme of schedule numbers exists which generally lists cars in chronological order. In this section those numbers are shown followed by the car's title. Cars described as "kitchen" contain a kitchen in addition to passenger accommodation and have gas cooking unless otherwise stated. Cars described as "parlour" consist entirely of passenger accommodation. Cars described as "brake" contain a compartment for the use of the guard and a luggage compartment in addition to passenger accommodation.

PULLMAN PARLOUR FIRST

Built 1927 by Midland Carriage & Wagon Company. 26/– 2T. Gresley bogies. 41 t. ETS 2.

| 213 | MINERVA | **PC** | BE | *BP* | SL |

PULLMAN KITCHEN FIRST

Built 1928 by Metropolitan Carriage & Wagon Company. 20/– 1T. Gresley bogies. 42 t. ETS 4.

| 238 | PHYLISS | **PC** | BE | | SL |

PULLMAN PARLOUR FIRST

Built 1928 by Metropolitan Carriage & Wagon Company. 24/– 2T. Gresley bogies. 40 t. ETS 4.

| 239 | AGATHA | **PC** | BE | | SL |
| 243 | LUCILLE | **PC** | BE | *BP* | SL |

PULLMAN KITCHEN FIRST

Built 1925 by BRCW. Rebuilt by Midland Carriage & Wagon Company in 1928. 20/– 1T. Gresley bogies. 41 t. ETS 4.

| 245 | IBIS | **PC** | BE | *BP* | SL |

PULLMAN PARLOUR FIRST

Built 1928 by Metropolitan Carriage & Wagon Company. 24/– 2T. Gresley bogies. ETS 4.

| 254 | ZENA | **PC** | BE | *BP* | SL |

PULLMAN KITCHEN FIRST

Built 1928 by Metropolitan Carriage & Wagon Company. 20/– 1T. Gresley bogies. 42 t. ETS 4.

| 255 | IONE | **PC** | BE | *BP* | SL |

PULLMAN KITCHEN COMPOSITE

Built 1932 by Metropolitan Carriage & Wagon Company. Originally included in 6-Pul EMU. Electric cooking. 12/16 1T. EMU bogies. ETS x.

| 264 | RUTH | **PC** | BE | | SL |

PULLMAN KITCHEN FIRST

Built 1932 by Metropolitan Carriage & Wagon Company. Originally included in "Brighton Belle" EMUs but now used as hauled stock. Electric cooking. 20/– 1T. B5 (SR) bogies (§ EMU bogies). 44 t. ETS 2.

280	AUDREY		**PC**	BE	*BP*	SL
281	GWEN		**PC**	BE	*BP*	SL
283	MONA	§	**PC**	BE		SL
284	VERA		**PC**	BE	*BP*	SL

PULLMAN PARLOUR THIRD

Built 1932 by Metropolitan Carriage & Wagon Company. Originally included in "Brighton Belle" EMUs. –/56 2T. EMU bogies. ETS x.

Non-standard livery: BR Revised Pullman (blue & white lined out in white).

| 286 | CAR No. 86 | **0** | BE | | SL |

PULLMAN BRAKE THIRD

Built 1932 by Metropolitan Carriage & Wagon Company. Originally driving motor cars in "Brighton Belle" EMUs. Traction and control equipment removed for use as hauled stock. –/48 1T. EMU bogies. ETS x.

| 292 | CAR No. 92 | **PC** | BE | | SL |
| 293 | CAR No. 93 | **PC** | BE | | SL |

PULLMAN PARLOUR FIRST

Built 1951 by Birmingham Railway Carriage & Wagon Company. 32/– 2T. Gresley bogies. 39 t. ETS 3.

| 301 | PERSEUS | **PC** | BE | *BP* | SL |

Built 1952 by Pullman Car Company, Preston Park using underframe and bogies from 176 RAINBOW, the body of which had been destroyed by fire. 26/– 2T. Gresley bogies. 38 t. ETS 4.

| 302 | PHOENIX | **PC** | BE | *BP* | SL |

PULLMAN PARLOUR FIRST

Built 1951 by Birmingham Railway Carriage & Wagon Company. 32/– 2T. Gresley bogies. 39 t. ETS 3.

| 308 | CYGNUS | **PC** | BE | *BP* | SL |

PULLMAN BAR FIRST

Built 1951 by Birmingham Railway Carriage & Wagon Company. Rebuilt 1999 by Blake Fabrications, Edinburgh with original timber-framed body replaced by a new fabricated steel body. Contains kitchen, bar, dining saloon and coupé. Electric cooking. 14/– 1T. Gresley bogies. ETS 3.

310   PEGASUS   x **PC** LS *LS* CL

Also carries "THE TRIANON BAR" branding.

PULLMAN KITCHEN FIRST

Built 1960 by Birmingham Railway Carriage & Wagon Company. Originally part of the National Collection. Rebuilt by Vintage Trains and returned to service 2021. Electric cooking. 26/– 1T. Commonwealth bogies. ETS x.

311   EAGLE   x **PC** VT *VT* TM

PULLMAN PARLOUR FIRST

Built 1960–61 by Metro-Cammell for East Coast Main Line services. –/36 2T. Commonwealth bogies. 38.5 t. ETS x.

325   AMBER   x **PC** WC *WC* CS
326   EMERALD   x **PC** WC *WC* CS

PULLMAN KITCHEN SECOND

Built 1960–61 by Metro-Cammell for East Coast Main Line services. Commonwealth bogies. –/30 1T. 40 t. ETS x.

335   CAR No. 335   x **PC** VT *VT* TM

PULLMAN PARLOUR SECOND

Built 1960–61 by Metro-Cammell for East Coast Main Line services. 347 is used as an Open First. –/42 2T. Commonwealth bogies. 38.5 t. ETS x.

347   DIAMOND   x **PC** WC *WC* CS
348   TOPAZ   x **PC** WC *WC* CS
349   CAR No. 349   x **PC** VT *VT* TM
350   TANZANITE   x **PC** WC *WC* CS
351   SAPPHIRE   x **PC** WC *WC* CS
352   AMETHYST   x **PC** WC *WC* CS
353   CAR No. 353   x **PC** VT   TM

PULLMAN SECOND BAR

Built 1960–61 by Metro-Cammell for East Coast Main Line services. –/24+17 bar seats. Commonwealth bogies. 38.5 t. ETS x.

354   THE HADRIAN BAR   x **PC** WC *WC* CS

5. LOCOMOTIVE SUPPORT CARRIAGES

These carriages have been adapted from Mark 1s and Mark 2s for use as support carriages for heritage steam and diesel locomotives. Some seating is retained for the use of personnel supporting the locomotives operation with the remainder of the carriage adapted for storage, workshop, dormitory and catering purposes. These carriages can spend considerable periods of time off the national railway system when the locomotives they support are not being used on that system. No owner or operator details are included in this section. After the depot code, the locomotive(s) each carriage is usually used to support is given.

CORRIDOR BRAKE FIRST

Mark 1. Commonwealth bogies. ETS 2.

14007. Lot No. 30382 Swindon 1959. 35 t.
17025. Lot No. 30718 Swindon 1963. Metal window frames. 36 t.

14007 (14007, 17007)	x	**M**	Chasewater Rly	LNER 61264	
17025 (14025)	v	**M**	CS	LMS 45690	

CORRIDOR BRAKE FIRST

Mark 2A. Pressure ventilated. B4 bogies. ETS 4.

14060. Lot No. 30775 Derby 1967–68. 32 t.
17096. Lot No. 30786 Derby 1968. 32 t.

14060 (14060, 17060)	v	**M**	TM	LMS 45596	
17096 (14096)		**PC**	SL	SR 35028	MERCATOR

CORRIDOR BRAKE COMPOSITE

Mark 1. ETS 2.

21096. Lot No. 30185 Metro-Cammell 1956. BR Mark 1 bogies. 32.5 t.
21232. Lot No. 30574 GRCW 1960. B4 bogies. 34 t.
21249. Lot No. 30669 Swindon 1961–62. Commonwealth bogies. 36 t.

21096	x	**CC**	CL	LNER 60007
21232	x	**M**	SK	LMS 46201
21249	x	**M**	SL	New Build 60163

CORRIDOR BRAKE STANDARD

Mark 1. Metal window frames and melamine interior panelling. ETS 2.

35317/322. Lot No. 30699 Wolverton 1962–63. Commonwealth bogies. 37 t.
35451–486. Lot No. 30721 Wolverton 1963. Commonwealth bogies. 37 t.

35317	x	**CC**	CL	Locomotives Services Crewe-based locomotives
35322	x	**M**	CS	WCRC Carnforth-based locomotives
35451	x	**CC**	CL	Locomotives Services Crewe-based locomotives
35461	x	**CC**	CL	Locomotives Services Crewe-based locomotives
35463	v	**M**	CS	WCRC Carnforth-based locomotives
35468	x	**M**	YK	National Railway Museum locomotives
35470	v	**CH**	TM	Tyseley Locomotive Works-based locos
35476	x	**M**	SK	LMS 46233
35479	v	**M**	CL	LNER 61306/LNER 60007
35486	x	**M**	BQ	LNER 60103

CORRIDOR BRAKE FIRST

Mark 2C. Pressure ventilated. Renumbered when declassified. B4 bogies. ETS 4.

Lot No. 30796 Derby 1969–70. 32.5 t.

35508	(14128, 17128)	**M**	BQ	LMS 44871/45212/45407

CORRIDOR BRAKE FIRST

Mark 2A. Pressure ventilated. Renumbered when declassified. B4 bogies. ETS 4.

Lot No. 30786 Derby 1968. 32 t.

35517	(14088, 17088)	b	**M**	BQ	LMS 44871/45212/45407
35518	(14097, 17097)	b	**G**	CS	SR 34067

COURIER VEHICLE

Mark 1. Converted 1986–87 from Corridor Brake Standards. ETS 2.

80204/217. Lot No. 30699 Wolverton 1962. Commonwealth bogies. 37 t.
80220. Lot No. 30573 Gloucester 1960. B4 bogies. 33 t.

80204	(35297)	**M**	CS	WCRC Carnforth-based locomotives
80217	(35299)	**M**	CS	WCRC Carnforth-based locomotives
80220	(35276)	**M**	NY	LNER 62005

6. 95xxx & 99xxx RANGE NUMBER CONVERSION TABLE

The following table is presented to help readers identify carriages which may still carry numbers in the 95xxx and 99xxx number ranges of the former private owner number series, which is no longer in general use.

9xxxx	BR No.	9xxxx	BR No.	9xxxx	BR No.
95402	Pullman 326	99350	Pullman 350	99673	550
95403	Pullman 311	99351	Pullman 351	99674	551
99040	21232	99352	Pullman 352	99675	552
99041	35476	99353	Pullman 353	99676	553
99052	Saloon 41	99354	Pullman 354	99677	586
99121	3105	99361	Pullman 335	99678	504
99122	3106	99371	3128	99679	506
99125	3113	99405	35486	99680	17102
99127	3117	99530	Pullman 301	99716 *	18808
99128	3130	99531	Pullman 302	99721	18756
99131	Saloon 1999	99532	Pullman 308	99723	35459
99241	35449	99534	Pullman 245	99880	Saloon 159
99302	13323	99535	Pullman 213	99881	Saloon 807
99304	21256	99536	Pullman 254	99883	2108
99311	1882	99537	Pullman 280	99885	2110
99312	35463	99539	Pullman 255	99887	2127
99325	Pullman 325	99541	Pullman 243	99953	35468
99326	4954	99543	Pullman 284	99966	34525
99327	5044	99546	Pullman 281	99970	Pullman 232
99328	5033	99547	Pullman 292	99971	Pullman 311
99329	4931	99548	Pullman 293	99972	Pullman 318
99347	Pullman 347	99670	546	99973	324
99348	Pullman 348	99671	548	99974	Pullman 328
99349	Pullman 349	99672	549		

* The number 99716 has also been applied to 3416 for filming purposes.

7. SET FORMATIONS

LNER MARK 4 SET FORMATIONS

The LNER Mark 4 sets generally run in fixed formations. Class 91 locomotives are positioned next to Coach B. Most Mark 4 sets were withdrawn in 2019–20, leaving eight rakes still on lease to LNER.

Set	B	C	D	E	F	H	K	L	M	DVT
NL06	12208	12406	12420	12422	12313	10309	11279	11306	11406	82208
NL08	12205	12481	12485	12407	12328	10300	11229	11308	11408	82211
NL12	12212	12431	12404	12426	12330	10333	11284	11312	11412	82212
NL13	12228	12469	12430	12424	12311	10313	11285	11313	11413	82213
NL15	12226	12442	12409	12515	12309	10306	11286	11315	11415	82214
NL16	12213	12428	12433	12467	12312	10315	11418	11318	11416	82222
NL17	12223	12444	12427	12432	12303	10324	11288	11317	11417	82225
NL26	12220	12474	12465	12429	12325	10311	11295	11326	11426	82223
Spare	12214									82205

TfW MARK 4 SET FORMATIONS

In 2021 Transport for Wales returned three shortened four-coach Mark 4 sets to service to replace its Mark 3 sets. They are used on selected services on the Cardiff–Manchester route and also to Holyhead, hauled by Class 67s. The sets are currently being lengthened to five-coach rakes using the spare Open Standard (Disabled) coaches listed.

Transport for Wales also purchased the four sets previously planned to be operated by Grand Central, plus another to make an eighth set and these were introduced at the start of 2023, mainly on the Manchester route. They are also to be lengthened to five coaches.

Set						DVT
HD01	12225	12315	10325	11323		82226
HD02	12219	12304	10328	11324		82229
HD03	12217	12324	10312	11325	12446	82216

Extra coaches to augment the above sets:
12447 12454

Set						DVT
HD04	12211	12310	10318	11319		82201
HD05	12224	12326	10321	11320		82200
HD06	12222	12323	10330	11321		82227
HD07	12210	12316	10301	11322		82230
HD08	12215	12308	10305	11316	12526	82220 *(currently out of service)*

Extra coaches to augment the above sets:
12434 12452 12461 12477

Spare 82204

TPE MARK 5A SET FORMATIONS

TransPennine Express operates sets of Mark 5A coaches hauled by Class 68 locomotives in push-pull mode, but introduction of these trains into service was very protracted. They are now mainly used between Scarborough and York/Manchester but are due to be withdrawn from service by TPE in December 2023.

Set	E	D	C	B	A
TP01	11501	12701	12702	12703	12801
TP02	11502	12704	12705	12706	12814
TP03	11503	12707	12708	12709	12803
TP04	11504	12710	12711	12712	12804
TP05	11505	12713	12714	12715	12805
TP06	11506	12716	12717	12718	12806
TP07	11507	12719	12720	12721	12807
TP08	11508	12722	12723	12724	12808
TP09	11509	12725	12726	12727	12809
TP10	11510	12728	12729	12730	12810
TP11	11511	12731	12732	12733	12811
TP12	11512	12734	12735	12736	12812
TP13	11513	12737	12738	12739	12813
Spare					12802

8. SERVICE STOCK

Carriages in this section are used for internal purposes within the railway industry, ie they do not generate revenue from outside the industry. Most are numbered in the former BR departmental number series.

BARRIER, ESCORT & TRANSLATOR VEHICLES

These vehicles are used to move multiple units, HST and other vehicles around the national railway system.

Barrier Vehicles. Mark 1/2A. Renumbered from BR departmental series, or converted from various types. B4 bogies (* Commonwealth bogies).

6330. Mark 2A. Lot No. 30786 Derby 1968.
6336/38/44. Mark 1. Lot No. 30715 Gloucester 1962.
6340. Mark 1. Lot No. 30669 Swindon 1962.
6346. Mark 2A. Lot No. 30777 Derby 1967.
6348. Mark 1. Lot No. 30163 Pressed Steel 1957.

6330	(14084, 975629)		**RO**	A	RO	LR
6336	(81591, 92185)		**FB**	A	GW	LA
6338	(81581, 92180)		**FB**	A	RO	LR
6340	(21251, 975678)	*	**RO**	A	RO	LR
6344	(81263, 92080)		**RO**	A	RO	LR
6346	(9422)		**RO**	A	RO	LR
6348	(81233, 92963)		**FB**	A	GW	LA

Mark 4 Barrier Vehicles. Mark 2A. Converted from Corridor First. B4 bogies. Lot No. 30774 Derby 1968.

6352	(13465, 19465)	**HB**	E		WS
6353	(13478, 19478)	**HB**	E		WS

EMU Translator Vehicles. Mark 1. Converted 1980 from Restaurant Unclassified Opens. 6376/77 have Tightlock couplers and 6378/79 Dellner couplers. Commonwealth bogies.

Lot No. 30647 Wolverton 1959–61.

6376	(1021, 975973)	**PB**	P	GB	ZG *(works with 6377)*
6377	(1042, 975975)	**PB**	P	GB	ZG *(works with 6376)*
6378	(1054, 975971)	**RO**	RO	RO	LR *(works with 6379)*
6379	(1059, 975972)	**RO**	RO	RO	LR *(works with 6378)*

Brake Force Runners. Mark 1. Previously used as HST Barrier Vehicles. Converted from Gangwayed Brake Vans in 1994–95. B4 bogies.

6392. Lot No. 30715 Gloucester 1962.
6397. Lot No. 30716 Gloucester 1962.

6392	(81588, 92183)	**Y**	CS	CS	ZA
6397	(81600, 92190)	**Y**	CS	CS	ZA

HST Barrier Vehicles. Mark 1. Converted from Gangwayed Brake Vans in 1994–95. B4 bogies.

6393. Lot No. 30716 Gloucester 1962.
6394. Lot No. 30162 Pressed Steel 1956–57.
6398/99. Lot No. 30400 Pressed Steel 1957–58.

6393	(81609, 92196)	**PB**	P	*GB*	ZG
6394	(80878, 92906)	**PB**	P	*GB*	ZG
6398	(81471, 92126)	**PB**	EM	*EM*	NL
6399	(81367, 92994)	**PB**	EM	*EM*	NL

Escort Coaches. Converted from Mark 2A (* Mark 2E) Open Brake Standards. 9419/28 use the same bodyshell as the Mark 2A Corridor Brake First. B4 bogies.

9419. Lot No.30777 Derby 1970.
9428. Lot No.30820 Derby 1970.
9506/08. Lot No.30838 Derby 1972.

9419		**DS**	DR	*DR*	KM
9428		**DS**	DR	*DR*	KM
9506	*	**DS**	DR	*DR*	KM
9508	*	**DS**	DR	*DR*	KM

EMU Translator Vehicles. Converted from Class 508 driving cars.

64664. Lot No. 30979 York 1979–80.
64707. Lot No. 30981 York 1979–80.

64664	**AG**	A	*GB*	ZG	Liwet	*(works with 64707)*
64707	**AG**	A	*GB*	ZG	Labezerin	*(works with 64664)*

EMU Translator Vehicles. Converted from Class 489 DMLVs that had originally been Class 414/3 DMBSOs. Previously used as de-icing coaches.

Lot No. 30452 Ashford/Eastleigh 1959. Mk 4 bogies.

68501	(61281)	**AG**	AF	*RO*	LR
68504	(61286)	**AG**	AF	*RO*	LR

Generator Vans. Former Nightstar Generator Vans converted from Mark 3A Sleeping Cars that are now used as carriage pre-heaters. Gangways removed. Two Cummins diesel generator groups provide a 1500 V train supply.

Lot No. 30960 Derby 1981–83. BT10 bogies.

96371	(10545, 6371)	**CA**	ER	IS
96372	(10564, 6372)	**EP**	ER	YA
96373	(10568, 6373)	**EP**	ER	YA
96374	(10585, 6374)	**IC**	ER	YA
96375	(10587, 6375)	**EP**	ER	YA

Eurostar Barrier Vehicles. Mark 1. Converted from General Utility Vans with bodies removed. Fitted with B4 bogies for use as Eurostar barrier vehicles.

96380/381. Lot No. 30417 Pressed Steel 1958–59.
96383. Lot No. 30565 Pressed Steel 1959.
96384. Lot No. 30616 Pressed Steel 1959–60.

96380	(86386, 6380)	**B**	EU	*EU*	TI

96381	(86187, 6381)	**B**	EU	*EU*	TI
96383	(86664, 6383)	**B**	EU	*EU*	TI
96384	(86955, 6384)	**B**	EU	*EU*	TI

Brake Force Runners or Universal Barrier Vehicles. Converted from Motorail vans built 1998–99 by Marcroft Engineering using underframe and running gear from Motorail General Utility Vans. Those operated by Colas Rail are often used in test trains and the Universal Barrier Vehicles have been fitted with Dellner couplers for use on multiple unit stock moves. B5 bogies.

Lot No. 30417 Pressed Steel 1958–59.

96602	(86097, 96150)	**MG**	MG	*RA*	KI	Henry
96603	(86334, 96155)	**MG**	MG	*RA*	KI	Oliver
96604	(86337, 96156)	**Y**	CS	*CS*	ZA	
96605	(86344, 96157)	**MG**	MG	*RA*	KI	Ernest
96606	(86324, 96213)	**Y**	CS	*CS*	ZA	
96607	(86351, 96215)	**MG**	MG	*RA*	KI	Philip
96608	(86385, 96216)	**Y**	CS	*CS*	ZA	
96609	(86327, 96217)	**Y**	CS	*CS*	ZA	

EMU Translator Vehicles. Converted from various Mark 1s.

975864. Lot No. 30054 Eastleigh 1951–54. Commonwealth bogies.
975867. Lot No. 30014 York 1950–51. Commonwealth bogies.
975974/978. Lot No. 30647 Wolverton 1959–61. B4 bogies.

975864	(3849)	**HB**	E		BU		*(works with 975867)*
975867	(1006)	**HB**	E		BU		*(works with 975864)*
975974	(1030)	**AG**	A	*GB*	ZG	Paschar	*(works with 975978)*
975978	(1025)	**AG**	A	*GB*	ZG	Perpetiel	*(works with 975974)*

LABORATORY, TESTING & INSPECTION COACHES

These coaches are used for research, testing and inspection on the national railway system. Many are fitted with sophisticated technical equipment.

Plain Line Pattern Recognition or Staff Accommodation Coaches. Converted from BR Mark 2F Buffet First (*) or Open Standard. B4 bogies.

1256. Lot No. 30845 Derby 1973.
5971/81. Lot No. 30860 Derby 1973–74.

1256	(3296)	*	**Y**	NR	*CS*	ZA
5971			**Y**	NR	*CS*	ZA
5981			**Y**	NR	*CS*	ZA

Brake Force Runners or Staff Accommodation Coaches. Converted from BR Mark 2F Open Standard. B4 bogies.

Lot No. 30860 Derby 1973–74.

5995	**Y**	NR	*CS*	ZA
6001	**Y**	NR	*CS*	ZA
6117	**Y**	NR	*CS*	ZA
6122	**Y**	NR	*CS*	ZA

Generator Vans. Mark 1. Converted from BR Mark 1 Gangwayed Brake Vans. B5 bogies.

6260. Lot No. 30400 Pressed Steel 1957–58.
6261. Lot No. 30323 Pressed Steel 1957.
6262. Lot No. 30228 Metro-Cammell 1957–58.
6263. Lot No. 30163 Pressed Steel 1957.
6264. Lot No. 30173 York 1956.

6260	(81450, 92116)	**Y**	NR	*CS*	ZA
6261	(81284, 92988)	**Y**	NR	*CS*	ZA
6262	(81064, 92928)	**Y**	NR	*CS*	ZA
6263	(81231, 92961)	**Y**	NR	*CS*	ZA
6264	(80971, 92923)	**Y**	NR	*CS*	ZA

Staff Coach. Mark 2D. Converted from BR Mark 2D Open Brake Standard. Lot No. 30824 Derby 1971. B4 bogies.

9481	**Y**	NR	*CS*	ZA

Test Train Brake Force Runners. Mark 2F. Converted from BR Mark 2F Open Brake Standard. Lot No. 30861 Derby 1974. B4 bogies.

9516	**Y**	NR	*CS*	ZA	*(works with 72616)*
9523	**Y**	NR	*CS*	ZA	

Driving Trailer Coaches. Converted 2008 at Serco, Derby from Mark 2F Driving Open Brake Standards. Fitted with generator. Disc brakes. B4 bogies.

9701–08. Lot No. 30861 Derby 1974. Converted to Driving Open Brake Standard Glasgow 1974.
9714. Lot No. 30861 Derby 1974. Converted to Driving Open Brake Standard Glasgow 1986.

9701	(9528)	**Y**	NR	*CS*	ZA	
9702	(9510)	**Y**	NR	*CS*	ZA	
9703	(9517)	**Y**	NR	*CS*	ZA	
9708	(9530)	**Y**	NR	*CS*	ZA	
9714	(9536)	**Y**	NR	*CS*	ZA	

Test Train Brake Coaches. Former Caledonian Sleeper coaches now used for staff accommodation in test trains. Fitted with toilets with retention tanks. Converted from Mark 2E Open Standard with new seating by Railcare Wolverton. B4 bogies.

9801/03. Lot No. 30837 Derby 1972.
9806–10. Lot No. 30844 Derby 1972–73.

9801	(5760)	**FB**	ER	*CS*	ZA	
9803	(5799)	**FB**	ER	*CS*	ZA	
9806	(5840)	**FB**	ER	*CS*	ZA	
9808	(5871)	**FB**	ER	*CS*	ZA	
9810	(5892)	**FB**	ER	*CS*	ZA	

Ultrasonic Test Coach. Converted from Class 421 EMU MBSO.

62287. Lot No. 30808. York 1970. SR Mark 6 bogies.
62384. Lot No. 30816. York 1970. SR Mark 6 bogies.

62287	**Y**	NR	*CS*	ZA	
62384	**Y**	NR	*CS*	ZA	

Test Train Brake Force Runners. Converted from Mark 2F Open Standard converted to Class 488/3 EMU TSOLH. These vehicles are included in test trains to provide brake force and are not used for any other purposes. Lot No. 30860 Derby 1973–74. B4 bogies.

72612	(6156)	**Y**	NR	*CS*	ZA	
72616	(6007)	**Y**	NR	*CS*	ZA	*(works with 9516)*

Structure Gauging Train Coach. Converted from Mark 2F Open Standard converted to Class 488/3 EMU TSOLH. Lot No. 30860 Derby 1973–74. B4 bogies.

72630	(6094)	**Y**	NR	*CS*	ZA	*(works with 99666)*

Plain Line Pattern Recognition Coaches. Converted from BR Mark 2F Open Standard converted to Class 488/3 EMU TSOLH. Lot No. 30860 Derby 1973–74. B4 bogies.

72631	(6096)	**Y**	NR	*CS*	ZA
72639	(6070)	**Y**	NR	*CS*	ZA

Structure Gauging Train Coach. Converted from BR Mark 2E Open First then converted to exhibition van. Lot No. 30843 Derby 1972–73. B4 bogies.

99666	(3250)	**Y**	NR	*CS*	ZA	*(works with 72630)*

Inspection Saloon. Converted from Class 202 DEMU TRB at Stewarts Lane for use as a BR Southern Region General Manager's Saloon. Overhauled at FM Rail, Derby 2004–05 for use as a New Trains Project Saloon. Can be used in push-pull mode with suitably equipped locomotives. Eastleigh 1958. SR Mark 4 bogies.

975025	(60755)	**G**	NR	*CS*	ZA	CAROLINE

Overhead Line Equipment Test Coach ("MENTOR"). Converted from BR Mark 1 Corridor Brake Standard. Lot No. 30142 Gloucester 1954–55. Fitted with pantograph. B4 bogies.

975091 (34615)　　　　　Y　NR　*CS*　ZA

New Measurement Train Conference Coach. Converted from prototype HST TF Lot No. 30848 Derby 1972. BT10 bogies.

975814 (11000, 41000)　　Y　NR　*CS*　ZA

New Measurement Train Lecture Coach. Converted from prototype HST catering vehicle. Lot No. 30849 Derby 1972–73. BT10 bogies.

975984 (10000, 40000)　　Y　NR　*CS*　ZA

Radio Survey Coach. Converted from BR Mark 2E Open Standard. Lot No. 30844 Derby 1972–73. B4 bogies.

977868 (5846)　　　　　　Y　NR　*CS*　ZA

Staff Coach. Converted from Royal Household couchette Lot No. 30889, which in turn had been converted from BR Mark 2B Corridor Brake First. Lot No. 30790 Derby 1969. B5 bogies.

977969 (14112, 2906)　　Y　NR　*CS*　ZA

Track Inspection Train Coach. Converted from BR Mark 2E Open Standard. Lot No. 30844 Derby 1972–73. B4 bogies.

977974 (5854)　　　　　　Y　NR　*CS*　ZA

Electrification Measurement Coach. Converted from BR Mark 2F Open First converted to Class 488/2 EMU TFOH. Lot No. 30859 Derby 1973–74. B4 bogies.

977983 (3407, 72503)　　Y　NR　*CS*　ZA

New Measurement Train Staff Coach. Converted from HST catering vehicle. Lot No. 30884 Derby 1976–77. BT10 bogies.

977984 (40501)　　　　　Y　P　*CS*　ZA

Structure Gauging Train Coaches. Converted from Mark 2F Open Standard converted to Class 488/3 EMU TSOLH or from BR Mark 2D Open First subsequently declassified to Open Standard and then converted to exhibition van. B4 bogies.

977985. Lot No. 30860 Derby 1973–74.
977986. Lot No. 30821 Derby 1971.

977985 (6019, 72715)　　Y　NR　*CS*　ZA *(works with 977986)*
977986 (3189, 99664)　　Y　NR　*CS*　ZA *(works with 977985)*

New Measurement Train Test Coach. Converted from HST TGS. Lot No. 30949 Derby 1982. BT10 bogies.

977993 (44053)　　　　　Y　P　*CS*　ZA

New Measurement Train Track Recording Coach. Converted from HST TGS. Lot No. 30949 Derby 1982. BT10 bogies.

977994 (44087)　　　　　Y　P　*CS*　ZA

New Measurement Train Coach. Converted from HST catering vehicle. Lot No. 30921 Derby 1978–79. Fitted with generator. BT10 bogies.

977995	(40719, 40619)	Y	P	*CS*	ZA

Radio Survey Coach. Converted from Mark 2F Open Standard converted to Class 488/3 EMU TSOLH. Lot No. 30860 Derby 1973–74. B4 bogies.

977997	(72613, 6126)	Y	NR	*CS*	ZA

Track Recording Coach. Purpose built Mark 2. BR Wagon Lot No. 3830 Derby 1976. B4 bogies.

999550		Y	NR	*CS*	ZA

Ultrasonic Test Coaches. Converted from Class 421 EMU MBSO and Class 432 EMU MSO.

999602/605. Lot No. 30862 York 1974. SR Mk 6 bogies.
999606. Lot No. 30816. York 1970. SR Mk 6 bogies.

999602	(62483)	Y	NR	*CS*	ZA
999605	(62482)	Y	NR	*CS*	ZA
999606	(62356)	Y	NR	*CS*	ZA

BREAKDOWN TRAIN COACHES

These coaches are formed in trains used for the recovery of derailed railway vehicles and were converted from BR Mark 1 Corridor Brake Standard and General Utility Van. The current use of each vehicle is given.

971001/003/004. Lot No. 30403 York/Glasgow 1958–60. Commonwealth bogies.
971002. Lot No. 30417 Pressed Steel 1958–59. Commonwealth bogies.
975087. Lot No. 30032 Wolverton 1951–52. BR Mark 1 bogies.
975464. Lot No. 30386 Charles Roberts 1956–58. Commonwealth bogies.
975471. Lot No. 30095 Wolverton 1953–55. Commonwealth bogies.
975477. Lot No. 30233 GRCW 1955–57. BR Mark 1 bogies.
975486. Lot No. 30025 Wolverton 1950–52. Commonwealth bogies.

971001	(86560, 94150)	Y	NR	*DB*	SP	Tool & Generator Van
971002	(86624, 94190)	Y	NR	*DB*	SP	Tool Van
971003	(86596, 94191)	Y	NR	*DB*	SP	Tool Van
971004	(86194, 94168)	Y	NR	*DB*	SP	Tool Van
975087	(34289)	Y	NR	*DB*	SP	Tool & Generator Van
975464	(35171)	Y	NR	*DB*	SP	Staff Coach
975471	(34543)	Y	NR	*DB*	SP	Staff Coach
975477	(35108)	Y	NR	*DB*	SP	Staff Coach
975486	(34100)	Y	NR	*DB*	SP	Tool & Generator Van

INFRASTRUCTURE MAINTENANCE COACH

Winterisation Train Coach. Converted from BR Mark 2E Open Standard. Lot No. 30844 Derby 1972–73. B4 bogies.

977869	(5858)	Y	NR	*DR*	Perth CS

INTERNAL USER VEHICLES

These vehicles are confined to yards and depots or do not normally move. Details are given of the internal user number (if allocated), type, former identity, current use and location. Many no longer see regular use. * = Grounded body.

041989*	BR SPV 975423	Stores Van	Toton Depot
061202*	BR GUV 93498	Stores Van	Laira Depot, Plymouth
–	BR NKA 94199	Stores Van	EG Steels, Hamilton
083602	BR CCT 94494	Stores Van	Three Bridges Station
083637	BR NW 99203	Stores Van	Stewarts Lane Depot
083644	BR Ferry Van 889201	Stores van	Eastleigh Depot
083664	BR Ferry Van 889203	Stores van	Eastleigh Depot
–	BR Open Standard 5636	Instruction Coach	St Philip's Marsh Depot
–	BR BV 6396	Stores van	Longsight Depot (Manchester)
–	BR RFKB 10256	Instruction Coach	Yoker Depot
–	BR RFKB 10260	Instruction Coach	Yoker Depot
–	BR Open Standard (End)12230	Training Coach	Network Rail York Rail Operating Centre
–	BR Open Standard 12415	Training Coach	Fire Service Training College, Moreton-in-Marsh
–	BR Open Standard 12417	Training Coach	Fire Service Training College, Moreton-in-Marsh
–	BR Open Standard 12443	Training Coach	Fire Service Training College, Moreton-in-Marsh
–	BR Open Standard 12468	Training Coach	Network Rail York Rail Operating Centre
–	BR SPV 88045*	Stores Van	Thames Haven Yard
–	BR NL 94003	Stores van	Burton-upon-Trent Depot
–	BR NK 94121	Stores van	Toton Depot
–	BR NB 94438	Stores van	Toton Depot
–	BR CCT 94663*	Stores Van	Mossend Up Yard
–	BR GUV 96139	Stores Van	Longsight Depot, Manchester
–	BR Ferry Van 889200	Stores Van	Stewarts Lane Depot
–	BR Ferry Van 889202	Stores Van	Stewarts Lane Depot
–	SR PMV 977045*	Stores Van	EMD, Longport Works
–	SR CCT 2516*	Stores Van	Eastleigh Depot

Abbreviations:

BV =	Barrier Vehicle	
CCT =	Covered Carriage Truck (a 4-wheeled van similar to a GUV)	
GUV =	General Utility Van (bogied van with side and end doors)	
NB =	High Security Brake Van (converted from Gangwayed Brake Van, gangways removed)	
NK=	High Security General Utility Van (end doors removed)	
NKA =	High Security Mail Van	
NL =	Newspaper Van (converted from a GUV)	
NW =	Bullion Van (converted from a Corridor Brake Standard)	
PMV =	Parcels & Miscellaneous Van (a 4-wheeled van similar to a CCT but without end doors)	
RFKB =	Kitchen Buffet First	
SPV =	Special Parcels Van (a 4-wheeled van converted from a Fish Van)	

9. COACHING STOCK AWAITING DISPOSAL

This list shows the locations of carriages awaiting disposal. The definition of which vehicles are awaiting disposal is somewhat vague, but often these are vehicles of types not now in normal service, those not expected to see further use or that have originated from preservationists as a source of spares or possible future use or carriages which have been damaged by fire, vandalism or collision. * = grounded body.

1201	TM	4849	CS	6179	CS	94101	CS
1252	SH	4932	CS	6324	CP	94106	BU
1253	SH	5179	TM	6351	BU	94116	BU
1658	CL	5183	TM	6360	NL	94153	WE
1679	RO	5186	TM	6361	NL	94166	BL
1696	YA	5194	TM	6364	CF	94170	CL
1800	RO	5238	CS	6365	CF	94176	BU
1883	CL	5331	FA	6412	CL	94195	BU
1954	CL	5386	FA	6720	FA	94196	CS
2131	CS	5420	TM	7204	CL	94197	BU
2833	CS	5478	CS	7931	BU	94214	CS
2909	CS	5631	BU	9440	SH	94222	CS
3051	YA	5657	BU	9489	CS	94227	HM
3060	CL	5710	CS	9490	BU	94229	CL
3241	CS	5777	BU	9496	DE	94302	CS
3255	FA	5797	RO	9529	YA	94303	CS
3277	RO	5815	SH	9531	WS	94304	MH
3279	BU	5876	SH	10222	BU	94306	HL
3292	BU	5888	SH	10242	BU	94308	CS
3295	RO	5922	WS	10257	BU	94310	WE
3309	TM	5924	WS	10530	ZN	94311	WE
3318	BU	5925	SH	10578	ZN	94313	WE
3331	BU	5928	TM	10588	ZN	94322*	CS
3334	KY	5954	BU	10656	ZN	94323	CS
3336	KY	5958	SH	11006	BU	94326	CS
3351	TM	5959	WS	11097	BU	94333	HL
3358	BU	5978	SH	12096	ZN	94335	CL
3368	FA	6009	SH	13508	RO	94336	CL
3379	KY	6029	SH	17013	ZG	94337	WE
3388	FA	6036	WS	18808	SH	94338	WE
3399	FA	6041	CS	35333	ZG	94401	CS
3400	BU	6045	SH	35467	CL	94410	WE
3408	CS	6073	SH	68505	ZG	94420	CS
3416	TM	6110	BU	80374	BL	94423	BU
3417	KY	6134	SH	80403	CS	94427	WE
3424	BU	6139	BU	80404	CS	94429	HM
4362	BU	6151	SH	80414	SL	94431	CS
4796	BU	6152	WS	92114	ZA	94434	CL
4799	BU	6154	SH	94058	BU	94445	WE

94450 WE	94538 CL	96170 CS	975687 CS
94451 WE	94539 CS	96178 CS	975688 CS
94482 CS	94540 TJ	96191 CS	975920 Portobello
94488 BU	94545 HM	99019 CS	977085 BU
94490 BU	94546 HL	99884 YA	977169 BU
94492 WE	94547 CS	975081 BU	977241 BU
94495 HL	94548* CS	975280 BU	977450 BL
94504 HL	95410 CS	975484 CS	083439 BU
94515 ZG	95727 WE	975490 BU	
94517 BU	95754 CS	975639 CS	DS70220 Western
94520 BU	95761 WE	975681 CS	Trading Estate
94522 CL	95763 BL	975682 CS	Siding, North Acton
94527 CS	96132 CS	975685 CS	Pullman 315 CS
94531 BU	96164 CS	975686 CS	Pullman 316 HN

10. CODES

10.1. LIVERY CODES

The colour of the lower half of the bodyside is stated first. Minor variations to these liveries are ignored.

AG	Arlington Fleet Services (green).
AL	Advertising/promotional livery (see class heading for details).
AR	Anglia Railways (turquoise blue with a white stripe).
AV	Arriva Trains (turquoise blue with white doors).
AW	Arriva Trains Wales or Arriva TrainCare dark & light blue.
B	BR blue.
BG	BR blue & grey lined out in white.
CA	Caledonian Sleeper (dark blue).
CC	BR Carmine & Cream.
CH	BR Western Region/GWR chocolate & cream lined out in gold.
CM	Chiltern Railways Mainline (two-tone grey/white & silver with blue stripes).
DR	Direct Rail Services (dark blue with light blue or dark grey roof).
DS	Revised Direct Rail Services (dark blue, light blue & green. Compass logo).
EA	East Midlands Trains revised HST (dark blue, orange & red).
EP	European Passenger Services (two-tone grey with dark blue roof).
FB	First Group dark blue.
FD	First Great Western "Dynamic Lines" (dark blue with thin multi-coloured lines on lower bodyside).
FS	First Group (indigo blue with pink & white stripes).
G	BR Southern Region/SR green.
GA	Greater Anglia (white with red doors & black window surrounds).
GC	Grand Central (all over black with an orange stripe).
GW	Great Western Railway (TOC) dark green.
HB	HSBC Rail (Oxford blue & white)
IC	BR InterCity (light grey/red stripe/white stripe/dark grey).
IS	BR ScotRail InterCity (as **IC** but with a blue stripe).
LC	New LNER Class 91+Mark 4 (oxblood, white & light grey with a red stripe).
M	BR maroon (maroon lined out in straw & black).
MG	Meridian Generic Rail (blue & grey with white lining).
MP	Midland Pullman (nanking blue & white).
O	Non-standard (see class heading for details).
PB	Porterbrook Leasing Company (blue).
PC	Pullman Car Company (umber & cream with gold lettering lined out in gold).
RB	Riviera Trains Oxford blue.
RC	Rail Charter Services (green with a broad silver bodyside stripe).
RO	Rail Operations Group (dark blue).
RP	Royal Train (claret, lined out in red & black).
SI	ScotRail InterCity (light grey & dark blue with INTER7CITY branding).
SR	ScotRail (dark blue with Scottish Saltire flag & white/blue flashes).
ST	Stagecoach {long-distance stock} (white & dark blue with dark blue window surrounds and red & orange swishes at unit ends).
TB	Transport for Wales all over black with a red logo.

TP	TransPennine Express (silver, grey, blue & purple).
V	Virgin Trains (red with black doors extending into bodysides, three white lower bodyside stripes).
VE	Virgin Trains East Coast (red & white with black window surrounds).
VN	Northern Belle (crimson lake & cream lined out in gold).
VT	Virgin Trains silver (silver, with black window surrounds, white cantrail stripe and red roof. Red swept down at unit ends).
XC	CrossCountry (two tone silver with deep crimson ends & pink doors).
Y	Network Rail yellow.

10.2. OWNER CODES

The following codes are used to define the ownership details of the rolling stock listed in this book. Codes shown indicate either the legal owner or "responsible custodian" of each vehicle.

125	125 Group
A	Angel Trains
AF	Arlington Fleet Services
AV	Arriva UK Trains
BE	Belmond (UK)
BN	Beacon Rail
BR	Brodie Leasing
CS	Colas Rail
DB	DB Cargo (UK)
DR	Direct Rail Services
E	Eversholt Rail (UK)
EM	East Midlands Railway
ER	Eastern Rail Services
EU	Eurostar (UK)
FG	First Group
GW	Great Western Railway
HN	Harry Needle Railroad Company
LF	Lombard Finance
LO	LORAM (UK)
LS	Locomotive Services
LU	London Underground
MG	Meridian Generic Rail
NN	North Norfolk Railway
NR	Network Rail
NS	Nemesis Rail
NY	North Yorkshire Moors Railway Enterprises
P	Porterbrook Leasing Company
PO	Other private owner
PR	The Princess Royal Class Locomotive Trust
RO	Rail Operations Group
RV	Riviera Trains
SP	The Scottish Railway Preservation Society
TL	Third Life Rail
TW	Transport for Wales
VT	Vintage Trains
WC	West Coast Railway Company

10.3. OPERATOR CODES

The two letter operator codes give the current operator (by trading name).
This is the organisation which facilitates the use of the coach and may not
be the actual Train Operating Company which runs the train on which the
particular coach is used. If no operator code is shown then the vehicle is
not in use at present.

BP Belmond British Pullman
CA Caledonian Sleeper
CR Chiltern Railways
CS Colas Rail
DB DB Cargo (UK)
DR Direct Rail Services
EM East Midlands Railway
EU Eurostar (UK)
GB GB Railfreight
GW Great Western Railway
LN London North Eastern Railway
LS Locomotive Services
NY North Yorkshire Moors Railway
PR The Princess Royal Class Locomotive Trust
RA Rail Adventure
RO Rail Operations Group
RS The Royal Scotsman (Belmond)
RT Royal Train
RV Riviera Trains
SP The Scottish Railway Preservation Society
SR ScotRail
TP TransPennine Express
TW Transport for Wales
VT Vintage Trains
WC West Coast Railway Company

10.4. ALLOCATION & LOCATION CODES

Code	*Depot*	*Depot Operator*
AL	Aylesbury	Chiltern Railways
BH	Barrow Hill (Chesterfield)	Barrow Hill Engine Shed Society
BK	Bristol Barton Hill	Arriva TrainCare
BL	Shackerstone, Battlefield Line	*Storage location only*
BO	Bo'ness (West Lothian)	The Bo'ness & Kinneil Railway
BQ	Bury (Greater Manchester)	East Lancashire Railway Trust
BU	Burton-on-Trent	Nemesis Rail
CF	Cardiff Canton	Transport for Wales
CL	Crewe LNWR Heritage	LNWR Heritage Company
CN	Castle Donington RFT	*Storage location only*
CP	Crewe Carriage Shed	Arriva TrainCare
CS	Carnforth	West Coast Railway Company
DE	East Dereham (Norfolk)	Mid Norfolk Railway
EP	Ely Papworth Sidings	*Storage location only*

FA	Fawley (Hampshire)	*Storage location only*
GA	Gascoigne Wood Sidings (S Milford)	*Storage location only*
HL	Hellifield	*Storage location only*
HM	Healey Mills (Wakefield)	*Storage location only*
HN	Hamilton (Glasgow)	Assenta Rail
IL	Ilford (London)	Greater Anglia/Elizabeth Line
IS	Inverness	ScotRail
KI	King's Norton (Birmingham)	SLC Operations
KM	Carlisle Kingmoor	Direct Rail Services
KR	Kidderminster	Severn Valley Railway
KY	Knottingley	DB Cargo (UK)
LA	Laira (Plymouth)	Great Western Railway
LB	Loughborough Works	UK Rail Leasing
LE	Landore (Swansea)	Chrysalis Rail
LM	Long Marston Rail Innovation Centre	Porterbrook Leasing
LR	Leicester	UK Rail Leasing
MA	Longsight (Manchester)	Alstom UK
MH	Millerhill (Edinburgh)	*Storage location only*
ML	Motherwell	Direct Rail Services
NL	Neville Hill (Leeds)	Northern
NO	Weybourne (Norfolk)	North Norfolk Railway
NY	Grosmont (North Yorkshire)	North Yorkshire Moors Railway Enterprises
PO	Polmadie (Glasgow)	Alstom UK
PZ	Penzance Long Rock	Great Western Railway
RD	Ruddington (Nottingham Heritage Railway)	125 Group
RO	Rowsley (Derbyshire)	Peak Rail
RS	Ruislip (London)	London Underground
SH	Southall (London)	West Coast Railway Co/Locomotive Services
SK	Swanwick West (Derbyshire)	The Princess Royal Locomotive Trust
SL	Stewarts Lane (London)	Govia Thameslink Railway/Belmond
SP	Springs Branch (Wigan)	DB Cargo (UK)
TJ	Tavistock Junction Yard (Plymouth)	*Storage location only*
TI	Temple Mills (London)	Eurostar (UK)
TM	Tyseley Locomotive Works	Vintage Trains
TO	Toton (Nottinghamshire)	DB Cargo (UK)
WE	Willesden Brent Sidings	*Storage location only*
WO	Wolsingham (Weardale Railway)	RMS Locotec
WS	Worksop (Nottinghamshire)	Harry Needle Railroad Company
YA	Great Yarmouth	Eastern Rail Services
YK	National Railway Museum (York)	National Museum of Science & Industry
ZA	RTC Business Park (Derby)	LORAM (UK)
ZB	Doncaster Works	Wabtec Rail
ZD	Derby Works	Alstom UK
ZG	Eastleigh Works	Arlington Fleet Services
ZI	Ilford Works	Alstom UK
ZJ	Stoke-on-Trent Works	Axiom Rail (Stoke)
ZK	Kilmarnock Works	Brodie Engineering
ZN	Wolverton Works	Gemini Rail Group
ZR	Holgate Works (York)	Network Rail